VARIETIES
OF CULTURE
IN THE OLD WORLD

ST. MARTIN'S SERIES IN PREHISTORY

Shirley Gorenstein and Robert Stigler,
General Editors

On the New World:

PREHISPANIC AMERICA
NORTH AMERICA

On the Old World:

THE OLD WORLD: EARLY MAN TO THE DEVELOPMENT
   OF AGRICULTURE
VARIETIES OF CULTURE IN THE OLD WORLD

Forthcoming:

A HISTORY OF AMERICAN ARCHAEOLOGY:
   METHOD AND THEORY

VARIETIES
OF CULTURE
IN THE OLD WORLD

Robert Stigler
Glynn Ll. Isaac
Barbara Isaac
Robert Rodden
Judith Treistman
J. Peter White

under the editorial supervision of
Robert Stigler

St. Martin's Press   New York

Library of Congress Catalog Card Number: 74-24979
Copyright © 1975 by St. Martin's Press, Inc.
All Rights Reserved.
Manufactured in the United States of America.
For information, write: St. Martin's Press, Inc.,
175 Fifth Avenue, New York, N.Y. 10010

The editors dedicate this series to
William Duncan Strong
who provided a standard of excellence
toward which his students continue to strive

PREFACE

This volume is one of a series whose aims are to give a succinct introduction to the study of prehistory and to sum up the present state of knowledge concerning prehistoric cultural developments in the significant archaeological areas of the Old and New Worlds.

The study of prehistory has been going on in an organized way for more than one hundred years. The results have been presented in thousands of papers, monographs, and books. Indeed, by the beginning of this century the amount of published information had become so vast that archaeologists found it hard to be prehistorians of the world. Space and time were divided up, and researchers became specialists in certain geographical areas and sometimes in certain periods. In recent years it has become even more difficult for one archaeologist to write a global prehistory. The would-be generalist today is hard-put to keep abreast of a whole field which is subject to radical technical and theoretical advances as well as a continuing explosion of information. Furthermore, the archaeologist always has a tendency to favor the area or areas where he has worked and to slight others of which he has no first-hand knowledge.

To overcome these problems, we have arranged for each of the first four books in this series to be written by a team of several authors, all of them specialists in one or more regions or time periods. The author of each chapter had a free hand, subject to limitations of space, in presenting his view of the present state of archaeological knowledge in his area. In none of the volumes or chapters has there been any effort to impose a Procrustean uniformity, other than in the general length and depth of treatment given to coordinate subjects. The authors have subscribed, however, to an overall organizational plan which is meant to give the series coherence as well as balance. This plan is primarily geographical, though some volumes and chapters also have temporal and topical aspects. The final book of the series, written by one of the editors with an introduction by the other, will be a history of archaeological method and theory in America.

We are indebted to Barry Rossinoff, who conceived the format of the series and saw the books' preparation through tumultuous times. We are also grateful to Judy Hammond, who worked with intelligence as well as artistry in preparing the drawings, and to Brian Hesse, Jim Nolan, and Thomas McGovern, who were innovative and indefatigable research assistants on the project.

SHIRLEY GORENSTEIN
ROBERT STIGLER

CONTENTS

VARIETIES
OF CULTURE
IN THE OLD WORLD

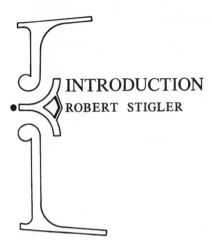

INTRODUCTION
ROBERT STIGLER

As the final quarter of the twentieth century begins, it might be possible to view the state of archaeology with some satisfaction. Since the end of World War II, thousands of sites have been excavated around the world. Scientific techniques of analysis have opened new horizons on the prehistoric past, providing an unprecedented range of information, and sophisticated theoretical frameworks that will enable us to interpret the evidence better are now being constructed. No large areas of the world remain total blanks; in some areas, great progress has been made in reconstructing and understanding past ways of life.

It is only natural that some parts of the world are less well known than others. Serious archaeological work began only in the nineteenth century; and selective factors, such as interest, accessibility, and availability of funds, led to early and intense investigations in certain areas while others were neglected. The detail in this volume's chapter on Europe, when compared to the chapters on Africa, eastern Asia, and Oceania, reflects the unevenness in data that has resulted. Still, given the variability of such factors as preservation, and culture history itself, we may expect eventually to have more comparable evidence from all parts of the world.

Although this positive view of modern archaeology is justifiable, few situations are perfect. Thus it is wise to indicate briefly for the general reader some of the shadows that most archaeologists today would also paint into the picture.

Popular interest in an academic subject is generally regarded as

1

a good thing. For scholars, there is the satisfaction both of public support and of sharing the interest and excitement of their findings. In this regard archaeology has never had to seek to stimulate public awareness; it has a certain built-in interest factor, for there is a great deal of genuine romance in the subject. The sheer intellectual —as well as physical—adventure involved in digging up and piecing together the evidences of the human past gives a kind of glamor to archaeology; this has been reflected in the public's response to archaeological discoveries since early in the nineteenth century. Moreover, the products of man's earlier arts and crafts—artifacts— are often fascinating, and not infrequently have considerable aesthetic appeal.

It is this aesthetic element, or rather its consequences, that spells trouble. To put it simply, serious archaeological research has always been plagued by an advance line of treasure hunters, sometimes clothed in respectability, but often, especially today, resorting to force and illegality—treasure hunters who feel no need for the preservation of scientific information, careful excavation, or the other factors that real archaeology depends upon.

Scientific study does not preclude an aesthetic appreciation of the objects of study. However, if aesthetic appreciation leads to the removal of archaeological objects from their context, it does foreclose any possibility of our understanding their full meaning. It is in this way—competition with collectors—that archaeology finds a significant portion of its evidence disappearing. Added to the unavoidable wear and tear that modern industrial society exerts on the archaeological landscape in many parts of the world, the deliberate looting of evidence is tragic. Archaeology is a subject with a very limited, exhaustible body of evidence to study, a supply which is endangered because of its wide popular appeal.

It is also often difficult for the interested public to evaluate what is said in the name of archaeology. Perhaps it is appropriate to be either bored or amused, rather than upset, by books and TV programs about flying saucers in ancient times. Unless we regard all fantasies as dangerous, little harm is done by them. On the other hand, sometimes more subtle or more plausible myths are propagated as archaeological truth. Again, owing to our ready interest in ourselves, our past, and our origins, various forms of either outright or discreet sensationalism can find a wide audience.

It is not *impossible* that archaeological evidence will someday show man originally to have been a "killer ape." He could conceivably have been an "oversexed ape," or for that matter he might turn out to have been a sweet, shy ape; but none of these interpretations has any basis in archaeological fact as yet. We are, however, regularly afflicted with journalistic rather than scientific versions of sensitive and important subjects such as the "nature" of man. Short of laboriously going back to the primary archaeological monographs to see what the known evidence really is, we are unable to evaluate such theses. Not many have the time or facilities to do this, and the myths persist.

Still more subtle are the attempts to depict prehistoric peoples as being more skilled than in fact they were. Prehistoric peoples need no apologies for or exaggeration of their abilities. Certainly, since Upper Paleolithic times began some 40,000 years ago we have all had the same kind of brain, and Cro-Magnon men and women could think as well as we do. The most conservative archaeological interpretations show a record of inventiveness everywhere, but it is foolish to credit peoples having still simple technologies with preternatural accomplishments, the construction of "Stone Age computers," or astounding feats of "conceptualization."

It is difficult to find a solution to this kind of distortion of archaeology. In a world addicted to flashy news and self-promotion, the only advice is to maintain a healthy skepticism in the face of extreme claims. Real archaeology makes a great deal of sense, and does not need sensationalism to be interesting.

Archaeologists must not be exempt from all criticism, and their part in the present unevenness of archaeological knowledge must be noted. As the various chapters of the volumes in this series illustrate, we have a detailed knowledge of some areas and periods, and only a limited knowledge of others. The present generation of archaeologists at home and abroad is well aware of the situation and we are in an era of better organization and catching up; but much work still needs to be done in several areas of the world.

There are many reasons for this unevenness. The study of prehistoric archaeology was born in Europe through what we may call the accidents of modern culture history; it has been pursued longer there than anywhere else in the Old World. Elsewhere, various political conditions and/or the vagaries of financial support for archaeological activities have affected the degree and kind of work done. But again—and here archaeologists themselves are accountable—the "glamor factor" has been at work; priorities have sometimes been set because a certain set of problems was fashionable. For whatever cause, fashions in archaeological work have always existed, and as Kent Flannery has recently observed, the "bandwagons" still roll. We hope, however, that none of the authors in this series is guilty of such sins.

This volume is designed for use with *The Old World: Early Man to the Development of Agriculture.* The division of chapters between the two volumes is mostly on a geographical basis. To a certain extent time differences are also involved. The first of these two volumes contains chapters on human evolution and on the Paleolithic era of the entire Old World. In this volume the chapters on Africa and Southeast Asia look at the local Paleolithic from a special viewpoint, while those on Europe, the Mediterranean, and the Far East take up at the beginning of post-Paleolithic times. Taken together, the two volumes are intended to provide general coverage of the prehistory and major archaeological problems of the Old World.

In "Africa," Glynn Ll. Isaac and Barbara Isaac shoulder the staggering task of condensing what we know about the prehistory of a whole continent into one chapter. Like most anthropologists, archaeologists, and historians writing on Africa, the Isaacs focus on Africa "south of the Sahara." This focus is based on the premise that however diverse the developments were in the southern nine-tenths of the continent, the culture history of the Mediterranean fringe of Africa was more different still, and really shared much more basically in traditions that extended beyond Africa. But the significant relations that existed between the north coast of Africa, including Egypt, and the rest of the continent are not ignored.

Even more forcefully than elsewhere, archaeological work in Africa has been affected by the modern (nineteenth- and twentieth-century) political history of the area. The net result has been that the African continent as a whole is still less well understood than any other world area of comparable extent. Even though interest in and promotion of archaeological activity differed from region to region during the colonial era, these were never more than minimal. The discoveries of the South African man-apes—the australopithecines—in the 1920s and 1930s stimulated great anthropological interest; later, the work of Louis and Mary Leakey in the 1950s and early 1960s established the equal anthropological importance of the East African area. Here again, the inherent drama in piecing together a picture of these remote beginnings of mankind from fragments of bone and crude stone tools has been a powerful attraction to legitimate archaeological and paleontological work, as well as to less than scientific speculation. At present, the overall result is that we are in the curious situation of beginning to understand more about the earliest days of human and cultural development than about most of the later stages in African prehistory. Most of the modern independent nations of Africa, however, are in the process of catching up in the pursuit of an understanding of regional prehistory and history, and thriving archaeological establishments with government support are developing widely.

Perhaps because of a lack of information, there has always been a tendency to regard Africa as marginal and noninnovative in its prehistoric development—a passive receiver of agriculture, stock herding, and other institutions from outside the continent. It is only recently that there have been suggestions of indigenous agricultural systems and complex political systems. As the evidence from Africa accumulates we can expect major contributions to be made to the picture of overall world prehistory and to our understanding of cultural processes.

Any attempt today to compress the prehistory of Europe into a single chapter faces different problems, as Robert Rodden's "Europe North of the Alps" shows. The wealth of archaeological detail available for Europe contrasts most sharply with the blank spaces and gaps in the sequences that still confront us in Africa. As stated earlier, Europe is the home of prehistoric archaeology. For well over a century, sound archaeological investigations carried out with consistently improving methods and techniques have been building up a fine-grained picture of the prehistory of the area.

In a sense, European archaeology north of the Alps has been blessed by the absence of the type of remains, "pyramids and palaces," which have sometimes functioned as distractions in the archaeology of the Near East, the Mediterranean basin, and other parts of the world where prehistoric studies have taken second place to classical or historical archaeology. From its beginnings European archaeology has been conducted within a sound intellectual framework. Problems facing the archaeologists here have resulted more from the intense occupation, cultivation, and general interference with the landscape that mark Europe, especially since the time of the Industrial Revolution. Archaeological work carried out within the traditions imposed by modern national boundaries has also fostered some problems in relating these different traditions. But taken together with Ralph Solecki's chapter on the Paleolithic in the earlier volume in this series, Rodden's "Europe North of the Alps" indicates the much more refined understanding that we have for this part of the world, and can as yet only strive for elsewhere.

In prehistory as well as in all later ages the Mediterranean basin seems to have been an arena for the interplay of the cultures of three continents. The distinctive topography and other physical features of the area have created an ecology, cultural and otherwise, that exists nowhere else. The complex interweaving of local and more widespread cultural features was in full force here from early prehistoric times.

In Rodden's chapter on "The Mediterranean" one can sense how the presence of the early Bronze Age civilizations in the eastern Mediterranean has at times affected the interpretations of Mediterranean prehistory elsewhere, and how the disentanglement of the different strands of cultural interplay is a basic, though unique, underlying problem. Although it has sometimes been argued that the Mediterranean basin was also a recipient more than an innovative area in prehistory, it is becoming clear, as Rodden shows, that such a simple picture is misleading, and that various local developments were afoot in the background during the middle periods of the ancient civilizations.

One could hardly choose a more difficult time than the middle 1970s to attempt to summarize adequately the prehistory of

China. After decades of neglect by all but a few prehistorians, Chinese and foreigners alike, the subject has been pursued with extreme vigor since 1949 in the People's Republic; but it is only now that distinct shapes are beginning to emerge from the evidence being uncovered. We will eventually have a body of archaeological material and interpretation of major magnitude to set alongside the work on the Near East, Europe, Africa, and the New World. The prospects in China are among the most exciting on the horizon of archaeology today.

In the past, attempts to make something of the still fragmentary evidence from China were based on outside models, borrowed from parts of the prehistoric world that were better known. Judith Treistman was one of the first to question some of these earlier assumptions, and her chapter on "The Far East" makes one realize the scope of the re-thinking that is now necessary in order to view Chinese prehistory properly. Set alongside some of the earlier, very simple treatments that we had become used to, this chapter has an altogether different quality that reflects the many new elements that must now be taken into account.

Far from Olduvai Gorge and Europe, this volume ends with the chapter on "Southeast Asia, Australia, and the Pacific," by J. Peter White. Archaeological work in this area has a pristine quality. It has been unencumbered by many of the historical and procedural problems that have affected prehistoric studies elsewhere, and although it has not been practiced as long here, archaeology has made great strides.

Certain themes and patterns unite the vast area culturally, while other elements show a sharp regional variation. The geographical fragmentation of the area into mainland and countless islands has, of course, affected its culture history even more than it has posed technical problems for modern archaeologists. The area has sometimes been judged marginal in reference to the mainstream of Old World prehistory, but White's chapter amply demonstrates the insights into general prehistoric processes which the archaeology of the area is providing.

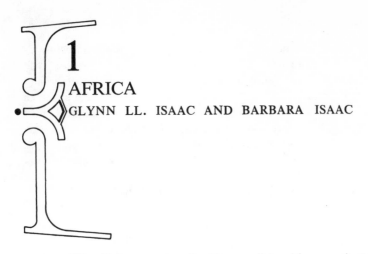

1
AFRICA
GLYNN LL. ISAAC AND BARBARA ISAAC

"Ex Africa semper aliquid novae" * said an ancient Roman, but the work of latter-day scientists, such as the Leakeys, Raymond Dart, and Desmond Clark, has shown that some of the most exciting things to come out of Africa are actually very old.

Darwin guessed that Africa might prove to be the evolutionary cradle of mankind; this insight has been extensively borne out by discoveries made during the past century. Certainly Africa is distinguished among continents for having the longest record of the fossil bones of our human ancestors and the longest archaeological sequence of the traces of their activities. Human prehistory in the African continent spans at least 2.5 million years, the first half of which constitutes a unique narrative of emerging culture. By about 1 million years ago, and perhaps before, men had spread to the adjoining continents of Europe and Asia. Finally, in the last few tens of thousands of years the dispersal of mankind was completed by penetration into Australia, the Americas, and Oceania.

Africa originally shared with adjoining parts of Europe and southwest Asia a broadly similar "family" of artifact traditions that are generally known as "Acheulian." Later, African culture, and indeed the cultures of each of the other areas, became increasingly more distinctive. Within Africa, too, a record of divergent regional and local material-culture traditions can be discerned. Despite complexity, and despite the existence of convergent as well as divergent trends, the record shows that culture varied

---

* "Always something new out of Africa."

in relation to major geographic zones. Following the metaphor of Sir Cyril Fox, one may regard the recurrent features of cultural geography as expressions of the "personality of Africa."

The limited scope of a single chapter precludes a full account of the complexities of a continent's entire prehistory. This account is therefore restricted to a summary of the unique early phases as well as a simplified sketch of the distinctive geographic patterns evident in later prehistory. In modern times the cultural borderland dividing Africa from Eurasia lies at the Sahara, and archaeology shows that this was the case through most of prehistory. The northern shores of Africa have long lain within the cultural sphere of the Mediterranean. Here, Mediterranean Africa is treated as a frontier rather than as an integral part of the continent.

• PALEOCLIMATE AND CHRONOLOGY

Until recently, it was widely assumed that the Pleistocene epoch was characterized by a moderately simple procession of three or four cycles of glaciation, each accompanied by global changes in climate. It was supposed that these dramatic events had great value as chronological markers, and that the meteorological changes had profound, obvious, and intelligible effects on culture history. These ideas arose in Europe. However, paleoclimatic history is so very complex, even in Europe, that the value of the suppositions is questionable; in Africa the assumptions are entirely inappropriate. Recent studies strongly suggest basic, long-term stability for African regional environmental regimes, with a complex pattern of short-term oscillations affecting balances among local micro-environments. Few of the fluctuations documented thus far can be correlated with those of other areas, and owing to the complex mosaic character of many African environments the effects of such fluctuations on man and culture are at present more or less incalculable.

The chronology used in this chapter and summarized in Chart 1.1 is based on geophysical age measurements and paleontological correlations. The principal labels used to describe African culture history are also shown. Many of these names are now known to cover odd assortments of only vaguely related entities, or to be unsatisfactory in various other ways. However, it is impossible to

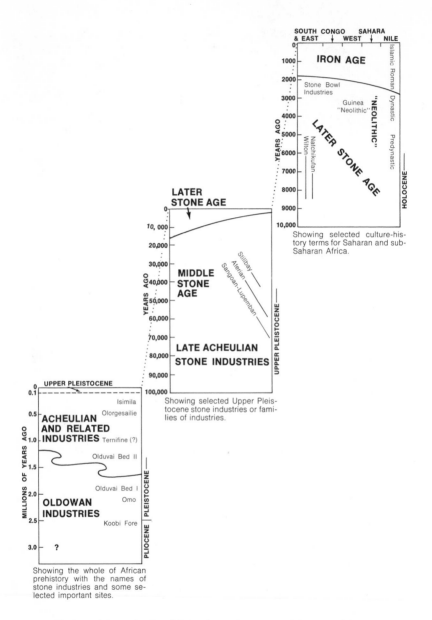

SOUTH CONGO SAHARA
& EAST ↓ WEST ↓ NILE

IRON AGE

Stone Bowl
Industries

Guinea
"Neolithic"

"NEOLITHIC"

Naichikulan
Wilton

LATER STONE AGE

Islamic Roman
Dynastic
Predynastic

HOLOCENE

YEARS AGO

Showing selected culture-history terms for Saharan and sub-Saharan Africa.

**LATER
STONE AGE**

Sillbay
Aterian
Sangoan-Lupemban

**MIDDLE
STONE
AGE**

**LATE ACHEULIAN
STONE INDUSTRIES**

YEARS AGO

UPPER PLEISTOCENE

Showing selected Upper Pleistocene stone industries or families of industries.

UPPER PLEISTOCENE

Isimila

Olorgesailie

**ACHEULIAN
AND RELATED
INDUSTRIES** Ternifine (?)

Olduvai Bed II

Olduvai Bed I

Omo

**OLDOWAN
INDUSTRIES**

Koobi Fore

?

MILLIONS OF YEARS AGO

PLIOCENE | PLEISTOCENE

Showing the whole of African prehistory with the names of stone industries and some selected important sites.

CHART 1.1   A simplified chronology of African prehistory.

avoid using them altogether, and most of the terms will continue to have some utility until they are replaced.

• THE EMERGENCE OF HUMAN BEHAVIOR

Africa is almost the sole source of evidence regarding the earliest phases of human behavior during the Lower Pleistocene. The distribution of the evidence shows that four areas are involved: (1) the Transvaal, (2) the Eastern or Gregory Rift Valley, (3) the Chad basin, and (4) northwest Africa (Figure 1.1*A*). Allegedly Lower Pleistocene "pebble tools" are reported from many other areas, but these have been omitted from this discussion because in most instances the dating is uncertain and the context such that the occurrences add little or no paleoanthropological information.

To understand the significance of the oldest archaeological evidence, the evolutionary background from which human behavior emerged must be considered. What are the most distinctive features of human behavior relative to the behavior of other primates? How can we recognize archaeological evidence of these distinctive activities? Answers to these questions are prerequisites for useful paleoanthropological studies of the Lower Pleistocene. The importance of Africa is greatly enhanced by the presence of a varied series of man's evolutionary relatives. Studies of the natural behavior of chimpanzees, gorillas, and ground-living monkeys, such as baboons, provide an invaluable perspective.

The data from comparative studies of primates are complex, but some critical points of contrast between apes and nonagricultural men can be identified and listed. Human behavior differs from that of the apes by involving (1) regular and systematic hunting (prior to agriculture), (2) the sharing of food within families or communities, (3) operation from well-defined "home bases," and (4) dependence on manufactured tools. All these features can be documented by archaeology.

Important but less archaeologically obvious features include: (5) the extensive division of labor between the sexes, (6) the existence of family units based partly on mating bonds, (7) the use of language, and (8) the regulation of behavior by complex rule systems known collectively as "culture." Inferences regarding

FIGURE 1.1   Early Pleistocene sites and stone tools.   (A) Sites of artifacts and hominid remains.

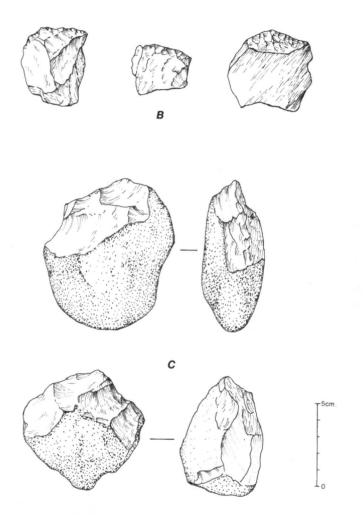

FIGURE 1.1 (Continued)   (B) Small Oldowan scrapers and flakes.
(C) Oldowan choppers.

these latter features will generally be indirect, and will depend on insight into functional interrelationships among classes of behavior that can be documented.

• THE TRANSVAAL CAVES: THE OLDEST TRACES OF HUMAN BEHAVIOR?

On paleontological grounds it is possible, but not certain, that three of the five major fossil-bearing sites in the Transvaal— namely, Taungs, Sterkfontein, and Makapansgat—are older than any of the archaeological sites yet studied in East Africa. These three are the sites that have yielded fossil specimens assigned to the "gracile" hominid species *Australopithecus africanus.* The other two anthropologically important sites, Swartkrans and Kromdraai, are definitely much less old (that is, Middle Pleistocene) and have yielded the "robust" hominid species *Australopithecus (Paranthropus) robustus,* along with another, more manlike hominid that may be *"Homo habilis"* or *Homo erectus.* In addition, the two latter sites have provided stone tools.

The work of Raymond Dart and the writings of Robert Ardrey have made the allegedly dramatic behavior patterns of *Australopithecus africanus* famous (or infamous, depending on how one looks at the matter). These workers have argued that these hominids were effective, ravening carnivores who also killed one another with moderate frequency. It has been further asserted that they made systematic use of animal bones, teeth, and horns as tools.

Given the upright stance and reduced canine teeth of *A. africanus,* the proposition that dependence on tools had already begun is eminently reasonable, as is the notion that these hominids were at least partially carnivorous. Unfortunately, the archaeological evidence that should provide the basis of behavioral reconstruction is either lacking or ambiguous. The hominid fossils were recovered either from commercial quarry operations or by means of paleontological excavations where little attempt was made to record the details of context. The tool-using hypothesis of Dart and Ardrey was based partly on surprising numerical patterns in the representation of bones from different parts of the skeletons of wild animals that were found with the hominid fossils. The patterns were attributed to the selection of certain bones by *A. africanus* for use as tools and weapons. It is now known that many aspects of these patterns are found among purely "natural" bone accumulations and have to do with differences in the durability of skeletal parts. We simply do not know for certain whether *A. africanus* hunted any of the animals among the bones of which his own are found. It is doubtful whether any of the cave sites were home bases, and C. K. Brain has argued convincingly that at least some of the hominid bones were carried in by leopards. At Sterkfontein, stone artifacts have been found in a pocket of deposits separate from those yielding the majority of *A. africanus* fossils. However, it is not yet clear what the evolutionary status of the fossils is, or whether the artifacts are significantly associated with them. Careful excavation by modern techniques has now been started at several of the sites. The results should help us to decide whether or not they document a stage in the evolution of human behavior that precedes the one already—and satisfactorily—reconstructed from East African evidence.

• SITES IN THE EASTERN RIFT VALLEY

The wealth of Early Pleistocene sites and fossils in East Africa can be attributed both to the favorability of the environment as a home for hominids and to the unique conjunction of geological circumstances along the Gregory Rift Valley. Fault subsidence of the valley floor creates lake basins which trap sediments. These in turn preserve fossils, often with a minimum of disturbance. Renewed earth movements intermittently break up old buried patches of sediment so that their contents are re-exposed for stratigraphic study and the discovery of fossils. These processes have been going on for more than 10 million years along a 600-mile gash in the earth's crust, thus creating an extremely complex geological record with an unparalleled wealth of hominid fossils. In addition, the volcanic activity associated with these processes has provided a number of rock forms that can be dated by potassium-argon determinations, thus providing a geophysical chronology for the fossils.

The oldest, well-studied evidences that indicate emerging human behavior come from Bed I at Olduvai Gorge in Tanzania. These are securely dated to 1.8 million years ago. The life work of Drs. Louis and Mary Leakey has established that the gorge cuts into stratified deposits containing the longest combined sequence of hominid fossils and archaeological sites that is yet known anywhere.

Fossils and stone tools are scattered in abundance throughout the strata at Olduvai; more significantly, they also occur together in concentrated patches. In a number of cases hominid fossils are also associated with these patches. The stone artifacts involved in these Lower Pleistocene sites are the products of comparatively unsophisticated craftsmen; but there can be no doubt that they were purposefully made. This is evident both from the forms of the specimens and from the fact that in some cases the rocks had been carried out onto lake flats which were otherwise devoid of stone. The artifacts from sites in the Bed I formation and the lower part of the Bed II formation at Olduvai constitute a related series to which the term "Oldowan Industry" is applied.

The interpretation of the hominid fossils that are associated with Oldowan sites is still the subject of debate among paleontologists. Two coexistent groups are widely recognized: *Australopithecus (Zinjanthropus) boisei* appears to be related to *A. (Paranthropus) robustus,* and differs markedly from a more gracile series often called *Homo habilis*. The earliest specimens of *H. habilis* at Olduvai have been likened by some workers to *A. africanus,* while late *H. habilis* specimens appear to be similar to early *Homo erectus* fossils. The fact of an evolutionary continuum, if it can be established, will in itself be much more important than the names assigned to arbitrary segments of that continuum. Archaeological evidence provides no definite clues as to which of the two hominid lineages made the tools and occupied the sites. It is not impossible that both did, although most workers would be prejudiced in favor of the gracile forms. The "robust" lineage disappears from the fossil record about 1 million years ago.

The animal bones clustered in association with artifacts span the full size range of the African fauna. On some sites, such as that of "Zinjanthropus," there is a tendency for small animals, including frog, tortoise, and rodents, and immature ungulates to be represented. However, other sites also have considerable quantities of the bones of species that range from rodents to pachyderms. Tools have been found with partially broken-up carcasses of an elephant and an extinct proboscidean, *Deinotherium.*

We have as yet no means for distinguishing bone assemblages accumulated by scavenging from those obtained by hunting; however, it seems likely that some hunting was always involved. It is interesting to note that while baboons and chimpanzees have been seen on occasion hunting, killing, and eating meat, they are not known to have scavenged meat even when it has been fresh and readily available.

We can now refer back to the behavioral questions that were raised earlier. The archaeological evidence seems to indicate that by about 2 million years ago or earlier in Africa, the behavior of some primate had undergone changes that greatly enlarged the importance of patterns fundamental to the repertoire of man. With reference to the list already set out: (1) tool making and a degree of tool dependence are documented at an intensity outside the known range for any ape; (2) meat eating was regularly practiced, and persistent hunting almost certainly took place; and (3) localities at which both discarded tools and bone refuse accumulated are most readily explained as home bases in the distinctive human sense.

These conclusions can be drawn directly from archaeological evidence; other important, though less readily documented, conclusions can also be made. The consumption of food at a home base involves transporting that food from the place where it was obtained. The quantities that can be estimated suggest that far more food was transported than was needed for feeding infants; thus extensive food-sharing seems an inevitable conclusion. Given the fact that paleontological evidence documents a prolongation of infancy even in the Transvaal australopithecines, it seems probable that some division of labor was established that differentiated males and the less mobile, child-encumbered females. In fact, the development of the home-based pattern really makes sense only in this context.

The archaeological evidence for these distinctive steps in the development of man's behavior patterns is entirely in accord with the paleontological evidence. The associated fossil hominids show distinct phylogenetic divergence from the apes, though we still do not know for certain how much further back evolutionary separation occurred. Estimates range from 3–25 million years ago.

The Oldowan tool kits that have been uncovered by Mary Leakey's careful excavations have proved to be much more diversified than had originally been imagined. In addition to a range of "chopper" forms, a varied series of small scrapers and beaked forms is found (Figure 1.1*B–C*). Anvils and hammerstones can be identified, and numerous unmodified but purposefully introduced stones are associated. It can be proved that the very numerous flakes present are not merely waste products from making choppers, as had long been assumed. The numbers of flakes and the differing proportions of rock types show clearly that these small sharp objects were a fully independent, and presumably an adaptively important, class of product. However, for all the variety, these industries show a certain basic simplicity: there are no very precise, recurring designs, and even the distinct types of choppers intergrade and show a high degree of opportunism in the use of primary forms. Put another way, the wide range of forms probably represents a wide range of functions, but the industries contrast with many later industries in the low degree of clear-cut differentiation and standardization of individual designs.

The Lower Pleistocene Oldowan sites thus provide unique documentation of the state of human behavior approximately 1.8 million years ago. Almost all the detectable, fundamental features of human behavior appear, either already present or incipient. Human evolution has involved interrelated changes of anatomical and behavioral systems. Thus it is scarcely surprising to find that from a stage very close to the outset of evolutionary divergence, the principal components of human behavior have functioned as an integrated complex, developing together. With this in mind it is tempting to hypothesize that the roots of language and of a social system incorporating male-female pair bonds, of however limited duration, were also present in the system at the Oldowan stage.

The suggestion that the fundamentals of human behavior were established in Oldowan times should not for a moment be taken to mean that there have not been important, even dramatic, subsequent changes. Any modern observer of the Olduvai scene might easily have been more immediately impressed by the "apeness" of what he saw. Yet apart from obvious things like the upright stance and tool making, a whole host of nonprimate patterns must already have been entering the behavioral repertoire. It is certainly a fact that nonhuman primates don't leave archaeological records, and that there *is* an archaeological record at Olduvai.

Recent exploration elsewhere in East Africa has begun to bring to light evidence of stages in human evolution antedating that of Bed I at Olduvai; the Lake Rudolf basin discoveries in particular are being made so fast that this chapter may be out of date before it is printed. Fragmentary hominid fossils dating from the Pliocene, 4–6 million years ago, have been found at Lothagam and Kanapoi; as yet the material is inadequate to determine in detail either the anatomy or the behavioral status of the hominids. At the Omo River delta in southern Ethiopia an international expedition directed by Yves Coppens and F. Clark Howell has explored a sequence of fossil-bearing sediments that spans a range 2–4 million years old. Numerous hominid teeth and more complete fossils have been found, especially toward the latter part of this time range. It appears that a "robust" and at least one "gracile" form are represented. In 1971 for the first time, tools and what may be an occupation site were exposed by excavation in the 2-million-year-old layers.

Along the east side of Lake Rudolf in Kenya, exploration under the leadership of Richard Leakey has resulted in the discovery of a vast area of fossil-bearing sediments spanning a time range from the Pliocene, 4.5 million years ago, to the early Middle Pleistocene, about 1 million years ago. More than forty hominid fossils have been found, including complete crania, mandibles, and post-cranial specimens. At least two varieties of hominid can be shown to have coexisted by about 2 million years ago. Excavations by one of the authors of this chapter, G. Isaac, in a tuff dated at 2.6 $\pm$ .26 million years, have yielded what are probably the oldest known tool kits and the oldest known home-base sites. The artifacts are in general like those of Bed I at Olduvai, but as yet no small scrapers have been found. Broken-up bones of a range of antelopes, pigs, and pachyderms are associated with the tools. The sites, which are perhaps 0.5–0.75 million years older than those of Olduvai, show much lower densities of artifacts and bone refuse. Perhaps this is indicative of lower intensities of tool-making, hunting, and food-sharing habits. It may indeed turn out that as we go back in time, the archaeological record will become fainter and fainter until it is imperceptible.

· THE ACHEULIAN IN AFRICA

It has already been pointed out that Oldowan stone craftsmen made varied tools, but that there is little clear evidence of exact, conventionalized designs being conceived and executed. In James Deetz's phrase, "mental templates" were vague, and perhaps even the ability to copy designs was rudimentary. Craftsmen designated as "Acheulian" began to make at least a few tool types according to some well-defined design rules. No matter what the raw material and what the exact manufacturing technique, hand-axes and cleavers have an unmistakable unity of convention.

There is evidence to suggest that the new forms were initially associated with the discovery of a new technique, that of striking very large flakes from boulders or blocks of stone. These flakes commonly are detached with very much the form of a hand-axe or cleaver. Whatever the case, the new, more specific designs appeared early in the Middle Pleistocene. Conventional estimates would put an age of around 500,000 years for the beginning of the Acheulian, but some potassium-argon dates from East Africa suggest that the age may really be more than 1 million years. Carbon-14 dates from the site of Kalambo Falls indicate that the Acheulian had come to an end there before 60,000 years ago. Whichever way scholars eventually agree to slice the geochronological pie, it is clear that the Acheulians continued in their way of life for an exceedingly long time. During this time the *maximum* standards of craftsmanship rose markedly. Upper Acheulian hand-axes may be exquisitely wrought objects with a symmetry and delicacy that were surely determined by aesthetic as well as practical motives, but the changes in form and refinement involved can also be measured and expressed quantitatively. (See Figure 1.2.)

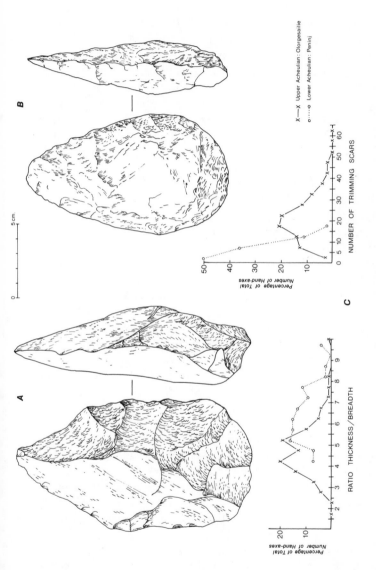

FIGURE 1.2   Early and late Acheulian hand-axes and their differences.   (A) Early hand-axe.   (B) Late hand-axe—thinner and more elaborately flaked than the early form.   (C) Frequency diagrams providing quantitative measurement of the differences.

Most of the unstandardized Oldowan varieties of tools continued to be made by the Acheulian stone workers. At Olduvai, Mary Leakey has shown that in upper Bed II "developed Oldowan" assemblages are found alongside Lower Acheulian assemblages. We do not yet know whether this indicates the temporal overlapping of two quite separate cultural systems, or unstable variability in artifact form from social group to social group, and from generation to generation; or whether the two kinds of assemblage represent "activity" differences in the tool kits of the same people at different places. A duality of aspect continues right through the Acheulian, in which assemblages dominated by hand-axes contrast with those dominated by informal scrapers (Figure 1.3). The latter variety were formerly known as "Hope Fountain" assemblages, a name now little used.

Hindsight shows us that "progressive" evolutionary changes in culture must have occurred during the vast time span of the Acheulian, but archaeology really only clearly documents the changes in technology such as those already mentioned. It may be that the Acheulians became more deadly and effective hunters than their Oldowan predecessors and that this involved higher levels of social cooperation and coordination. The elephant-killing locale at Torralba-Ambrona in Spain is certainly without parallel in the Oldowan record, but it is also unique among Acheulian sites—a maximum, not a norm. One African site also provides good evidence of moderately intensive cooperative hunting: at Olorgesailie in Kenya, a dense concentration of Acheulian tools was associated with the broken-up bones of more than fifty individuals of an extinct, gigantic species of baboon. Baboons are social animals and it seems probable that they could have been systematically hunted only by a coordinated group. One paleontologist has suggested that the hunting prowess of the African Acheulians during the Middle Pleistocene was sufficient to bring about the extermination of numerous mammal species. The evidence is as yet inconclusive, but the possibility is an interesting one. The same suggestion has been made with regard to Paleo-Indian hunters in the New World in late Pleistocene times.

The paucity of bone on several African sites, where it would have been preserved if present, serves to draw attention to the fact that men were not purely carnivorous. Human adaptation also included the use of vegetable food which was probably gathered by women to serve as a safeguard against failure in the hunt.

Africa has been the center of numerous studies aimed at investigating the relations between ecology, economy, and social groupings during the Middle Pleistocene. The movement that began in 1943 with Mary Leakey's excavations at Olorgesailie has since come to include a series of camp sites dug in the sedimentary basins at Olduvai, Isimila, Kalambo Falls, Baringo, Nsongezi, and Melka Kontoure. As yet most of the information from these excavations cannot readily be translated from artifact technicalities into paleoanthropology, but the progress of this work can be expected to provide insight into the critical formative developments in culture and economy that must have occurred during the Middle Pleistocene.

• CULTURAL SPEED-UP

The lives of Acheulian people were far from dull. Recent studies show that hunter-gatherers, like other carnivores, enjoy large amounts of leisure time. Men in prehistory certainly experienced both the rigors and the thrills of hunting, as well as the hazard of being the potential prey of other carnivores. From time to time social tensions among men were probably an added danger. Since aggressive or violent encounters are a part of primate behavior, and are also observable in most contemporary human societies, it would be unwarranted to imagine a paradisiacal situation for the intermediate phases of human evolution.

Individual lives may have been eventful, but significant culture change was immeasurably slow, and probably had a random rather than a directional aspect. Perhaps this can be attributed to the combined effects of the physiological restraints of insufficiently evolved brains and to the comparative simplicity of early cultural and linguistic systems. Whatever the reason, a threshold in psychological and cultural evolution had evidently been crossed by the Upper Pleistocene, and thereafter things began to speed up in Africa and all over the world. Perhaps for the first time, population pressures may have been a factor, but this is hard to assess.

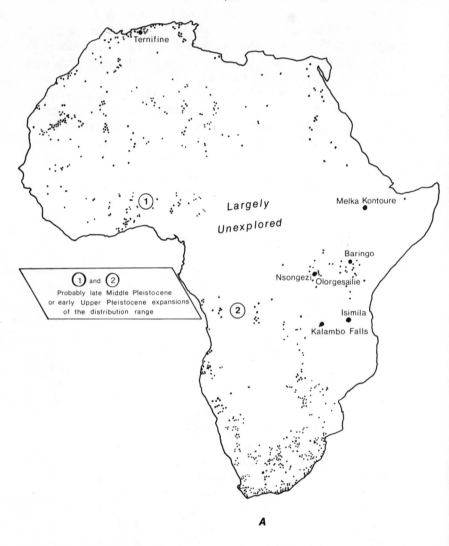

FIGURE 1.3   Acheulian tools.   (A) Distribution of sites.

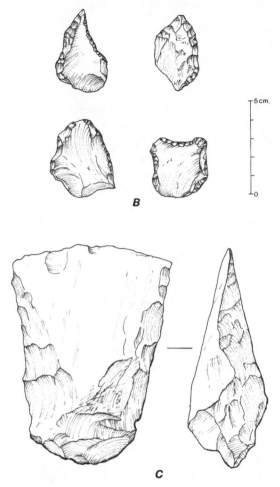

FIGURE 1.3 (Continued)   (B) Small scrapers and borers.   (C) Cleaver.

One would guess that evolving language systems also played a critical role.

Acheulian and Oldowan sites in Africa occur mainly in the savannah arc that encircles the more densely vegetated Congo basin and West Africa. Acheulian sites are also numerous in parts of the Sahara, but may belong to climatic phases when savannah or "steppe" conditions prevailed there. Certainly during the Middle Pleistocene there are no signs of material-culture differentiation in relation to geographic zones outside the wide range of savannah environments. During the Upper Pleistocene the first differentiation did occur, and at least three geographically segregated groups of stone artifact assemblages came into existence. Each of these groups of assemblages shows wide internal variation; however, there are also internal family resemblances that suggest relationships. Each of the groups has a different and partly complementary distribution pattern in relation to each of the others. Perhaps it is legitimate to think of these groups as representing paleoculture areas, using that term with some of the connotations developed by ethnographers in the New World, but without being too precise about its definition. (For a map of the areas, see Figure 1.4A.)

The three culture areas can first be distinguished in the time period around thirty to forty thousand years ago. Despite growing complexity and great change, they have remained the centers of culturally distinct divisions of Africa, and a case can be made that they continue to be reflected in recent ethnographic patterns of culture.

The group of stone-tool industries that is associated with the Congo culture area is generally known as "Sangoan," but since there is evidence that the Sangoan may be indivisible from the "Lupemban" industrial complex that was formerly supposed to succeed it, the term "Sangoan-Lupemban" is used here. These industries are characterized by a distinctive series of comparatively large stone tools. In some assemblages these are strikingly crude, especially in those believed to be early, or the so-called true Sangoan. Other assemblages such as the "true" Lupemban are characterized by "core-axes" which are neat oval or subrectangular bifacial tools which would have made serviceable adzes or hoes. Thin, bifacial, leaf-shaped implements range in size from pieces that might have been daggers or machetes to those that were probably projectile points. Flake and smaller scraper components of the industry are numerous and fairly generalized, with a low incidence of the "Levallois" technique. Examples of Sangoan-Lupemban tools are shown in Figure 1.4*B–D*.

This Sangoan-Lupemban material-culture tradition probably arose among Upper Pleistocene Acheulian groups which penetrated the geographically and ecologically distinct regions of the Congo basin for the first time. The Acheulian industries of this region are probably all of comparatively late date and show a suggestive tendency to heavy, crude, hand-axe forms.

J. D. Clark has put forward the idea that the shift in artifact form is a consequence of movement into more heavily wooded areas. Ethnographic and experimental information indicates that the heavier part of the stone equipment may have been serviceable for woodworking or for opening the hives of wild bees in search of honey. However, direct evidence that the tools were so used is lacking. This line of explanation of the adaptation of a tool kit should not be regarded as necessarily deterministic. Almost all primitive peoples, even those of the desert, engage in shaping wood. Some develop elaborate, differentiated tools for this; others do not. It is presumably in part an accident of culture history that the peoples of this culture area do appear to have initiated a tradition of distinctive woodworking tool kits.

Up to the present, no Sangoan-Lupemban sites have ever been found where satisfactory economic or ecological data have been preserved. Fossilized bone is exceedingly rare in the heavily weathered soils and sediments of the moist equatorial regions of this culture area, so nothing is known about the degree of reliance that Sangoan-Lupemban people placed on hunting. The projectile points are suggestive of hunting activity. Elephant and hippopotamus, although hard to kill, are important protein prizes for pygmy hunters in part of the area today, and this may also have been true in the past. A great variety of wild vegetable foods and honey are available in this broad ecological zone, and it seems likely that these would have been important or preponderant in day-to-day subsistence.

Meanwhile an equally distinct set of related stone-craft tradi-

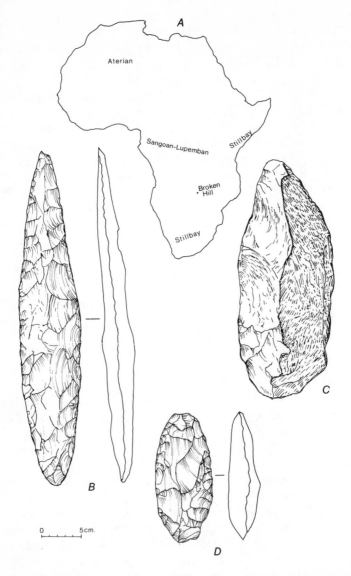

FIGURE 1.4   Three distinct culture areas in the Upper Pleistocene.
(A) Map of the areas.   *(B–D)* Sangoan-Lupemban tools: *B*, Lanceo-
late point; *C*, Heavy pick; *D*, Core-axe.

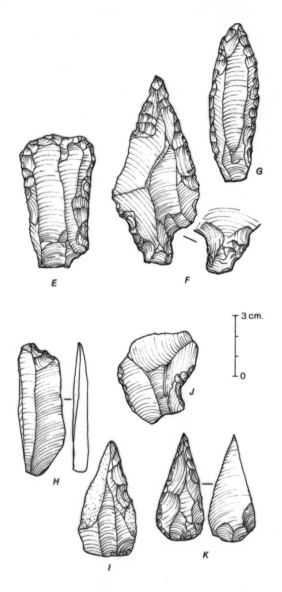

FIGURE 1.4 (Continued)   (E–G) Aterian tools: E, Scraper; F, End-scraper; G, Mousterian-like tool.   (H–K) Stillbay tools: H, I, and J, Retouched blades and flakes; K, Partially bifacial point.

tions had developed in a markedly contrasting ecological zone: the Sahara. The name "Aterian" (Figure 1.4*E–G*) is given to a set of tool assemblages that are distinguished among other things by the stylistic trick of making tools with tangs or stems. Tangs were an Aterian obsession; at times, the craftsmen appear to have been supremely skilled in the technique: tangs were put on all sorts of tools other than the projectile points for which a stem seems most appropriate.

Aterian tool-making traditions appear to have arisen around forty or fifty thousand years ago out of a "Mousterian" milieu in northwest Africa. The industries have a Middle Paleolithic disc-core and Levallois-core technological base, but they are in part contemporary with Upper Paleolithic industries in the Mediterranean basin, and in some instances assemblages include Upper Paleolithic tool forms. Aterian stone-craft traits are distributed over most of the Sahara, ranging from the Moroccan coast almost to the Nile Valley, and from the Mediterranean coast south towards the sudanic belt at latitude 15° N.

Dates range from greater than 32,000 to less than 10,000 years ago. Assemblages representing samples from this vast segment of space-time are by no means identical; but they show degrees of relationship that are usefully summarized by their collective inclusion in a single culture area.

Even if allowance is made for cooler and moister conditions in the Sahara at times during the last ice age, environments over most of the Aterian culture area would at best have been dry and steppe-like, and it is clear that Aterian cultures were adapted to such conditions. It would be absurd to suppose that the Aterian tang itself is a direct adaptation to desert life; rather, adaptation must have consisted of a fund of expertise concerning animal movements and the location of seasonably available plants and small animals that could be gathered as foods. Perhaps, however, the shared tang-making habit and other stone-craft traits do symbolize a certain community of lore and tradition about how to live in an area throughout which the environment is essentially the same; such is the nature of a culture area. Aterian industries and their distribution are known largely from surface collections. There is regrettably little direct evidence concerning subsistence patterns.

In the Maghreb of northwest Africa, stone tools of Aterian tradition ceased to be made around 12–14 thousand years ago, and tool kits involving numerous little blade implements were produced. This new series of Upper and epi-Paleolithic industries appears to have its closest relationships with other industries along the north coast, in the Nile Valley and in Palestine. It is uncertain how long Aterian traditions lasted elsewhere in the Sahara: in some areas there are no traces of industries between the local Aterian and the local "Neolithic." Either the Aterian lingered on into the Holocene or the areas became depopulated for a time.

At the southern edges of the Aterian culture area there are features of the stone-tool assemblages that may be indicative of interaction with the Sangoan-Lupemban area; for example, foliate bifacial points are relatively prominent. It is also true that tanged projectile points began to be made in the Congo basin about 11,000 years ago; this may or may not be due to chance. Until the intervening area is studied the reality and extent of interaction cannot be fairly judged. Outside the Aterian and Sangoan-Lupemban areas lie two other major regions. One is the sudanic belt; this, especially its eastern end, is archaeologically one of the least known portions of Africa. The other region lies along what can be called the backbone of Africa, a series of highlands and plateaus that run from Ethiopia to South Africa. This strip is extremely variegated with complex mosaics of steppe, savannah, woodland, and forest environments.

This is part of the savannah arc that contains all the known Lower and early Middle Pleistocene sites and most of the later Acheulian sites. During the subsequent period of the Upper Pleistocene, resemblances among industries along the eastern backbone are less clear than those linking assemblages in the Aterian or Sangoan-Lupemban areas. For the sake of tidiness, a third area, the eastern or "Stillbay" culture area, can be reported here, but certainly several geographically smaller units will eventually be necessary to describe cultural and ecological history adequately.

The main features linking eastern and southern African industries of this time period are negative: the industries lack the specific characteristics of industries in either of the other two areas. Weak positive similarities are found in the tendency to a stronger Levalloisian technical component than is normal in the Sangoan-Lupemban, and in the tendency for the eastern industries to include bifacial, foliate, projectile points—"Stillbay" points, a feature that is also known in both other culture areas at this time. These tools are illustrated in Figure 1.4*H–K*.

It has been supposed that a transitional stage between the Late Acheulian and the Upper Pleistocene cultures existed. However, reliable evidence for this "First Intermediate" or Fauresmith division has proved elusive.

Late Upper Pleistocene industries in the eastern culture area are often referred to as Middle Stone Age, a category into which the contemporary Sangoan-Lupemban may also be placed. A number of human fossils belonging to this time period, and cultural division, have been found. The best-known group is represented in eastern, central, and southern Africa and is often called Rhodesioid, after the almost complete skull found at Broken Hill in Zambia, then Northern Rhodesia. These fossil skulls have brain cases fully as large as those of modern men, but like the Neandertals in Europe, have their own brand of cranial morphology, including markedly thick bones, prominent brows, and large faces.

Bones preserved at a number of sites show that Middle Stone Age men were effective hunters who bagged animals ranging from the pachyderms down to rodents; however, there is not yet sufficient evidence to compare their efficacy with that of their Acheulian predecessors. Gathered vegetal food was probably of great importance as it is for all tropical and warm-temperate hunting peoples.

• AFRICA IN RELATION TO THE WORLD AT LARGE

After taking a close look at the features of three cultural areas within Africa, one can also look at the larger scene: Africa as a whole and Africa in the larger world. The African industries of late Pleistocene times have in common the fact of a Levalloisian, or prepared-core, technical basis for stone craft. At the time of the inception of these cultures, about forty to seventy thousand years ago, this feature was also held in common with the various Mousterian industries of the Mediterranean basin.

After the period thirty to forty thousand years ago, the Levallois-based industries were replaced in the Mediterranean by blade and burin industries of the Upper Paleolithic; in Africa, Levallois methods continued in use. However, there are reasons for believing that the continent did continue to participate in certain general developments: in Africa as in many other regions there was a widespread, but not universal, tendency to reduction in average tool size; the cultural speed-up continued in Africa as elsewhere with increasing rates of local cultural divergence and increasing rates of stylistic and other change within each region.

Recent researches have shown that during the Late Pleistocene the Egyptian portion of the Nile Valley was part of the Mediterranean "blade" province. Unusual cultural complexities have been demonstrated there, as well as the oldest evidence of group warfare: a cemetery with more than 60 percent of the bodies showing signs of death by weapons. It is possible that the confines of the Nile Valley produced an almost experimental microcosm in which population pressure on the narrow strip of resources encouraged intergroup competition and cultural differentiation. Perhaps the larger-scale phenomena of differentiation and speed-up in Africa and the rest of the world are similarly related to less extreme, but real, pressures.

There is also growing evidence that blade and backed "microlith" forms were sometimes made in sub-Saharan Africa well back in the so-called Middle Stone Age.

• POST-PLEISTOCENE HUNTER-GATHERERS

This period, which is often known as the Later Stone Age, begins at the very end of the Pleistocene. It provides clear evidence of the fact that Africa continued to participate in the broad cultural trends of the Old World, because in Africa, as elsewhere, the pattern of stone tool kits was transformed by the rising importance of small implements with blunted backs, the so-called microliths. The three culture areas partially preserved their separate identities, but also underwent parallel changes in this regard. It has been suggested that the spread of microlithic tool habits is related to the spread of a critical invention: the bow and arrow. This is a plausible idea inasmuch as the use of the bow did spread at about this time; however, the hypothesis is not yet proven.

The distribution of sites for the Later Stone Age is shown in Figure 1.5*A*.

The Saharan cultural area may have been largely depopulated

FIGURE 1.5   Later Stone Age hunting-gathering cultures.   (A) Distribution of sites for hunting-gathering and some contemporary cultures.

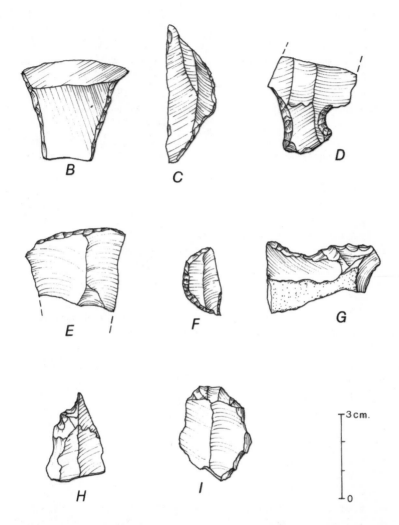

FIGURE 1.5 (Continued)   (B–E) Tshitolian tools from Angola: *B,*
Tranchet; *C,* Microlithic crescent; *D,* Tanged projectile point; *E,* Trun-
cated flake.   (F–I) Wilton tools from Zambia: *F,* Microlithic crescent;
G, Denticulate scraper; *H,* Small borer; *I,* Small scraper.

during the first part of this time period, though later during the
period, five to ten thousand years ago, a series of shallow playa
lakes formed along its southern margins. Hunter-fishers who used
harpoons made with barbed bone points and who made microliths lived around the shores of these lakes. Their material culture
shows obvious resemblances to tool kits in use along the Nile at
the same time, and the harpoon trait also has a contemporaneous
distribution up the White Nile to Lake Rudolf and the Eastern
Rift Valley, and to Lake Albert in the Western Rift. The stone
industries associated with the harpoons are rather different in
each case.

In the Congo area, despite change, continuity is well established.
The characteristic core-axe of the Sangoan-Lupemban continued
to be made, though the size norm grew steadily smaller. New forms
were added to the tool kit, notably tanged bifacial points, splayed
U- or V-shaped *tranchets,* and geometric microliths. Industries belonging to the later microlithic stages of this continuum are generally known as "Tshitolian," and date from eleven to two or three
thousand years ago. (See Figure 1.5*B–E.*)

Along the eastern spine of Africa a diverse series of microlithic
industries are known that are only similar by virtue of the promi-
nence of crescent microliths in all of them, and of small, thumb-
nail-sized and -shaped scrapers in some of them (Figure 1.5*F–I*).
They have all been included in the "Wilton" culture, but it
is clear from current research that many somewhat different industries are involved. In some regions it can be shown that transitional
assemblages exist between the Stillbay and Wilton industries. These
may combine diminutive Levallois cores and small projectile points
with the manufacture of bladelets and microliths. Such industries
have generally been termed "Second Intermediate" or "Magosian."
Unfortunately, it has been discovered that the type series at Magosi
was a deceptive mixture of Middle and Later Stone Age material,
not a transition phase. This is not, however, true of all such com-
binations. Wilton assemblages sometimes include neat bone tools
and commonly include ostrich eggshell beads. Late assemblages
may include pottery and various ground stone objects. In some
areas there is strong circumstantial evidence that Wilton peoples
were among the artists who painted the walls of rock shelters with

naturalistic representations that have become famous as "Bushman art."

In central Africa, particularly northern Zambia and Malawi, a rather distinctive set of microlithic assemblages has been classified apart as the "Natchikufan" culture. Distinctive Later Stone Age artifacts also occur on the central plateau of South Africa, where they are known as "Smithfield," but most of the material was recovered from surface sites, and recent research suggests that the term will have to be abandoned because a mixture of tool kits is involved.

Bone is preserved at many Wilton sites; it is clear that some peoples of this period were extremely successful as hunters. Excavations at Gwisho in Zambia have recovered large quantities of bone, but food plant remains are also prominent. Sites such as this serve to confirm the view that for nonagricultural peoples in the tropics, gathered vegetable foods are very important.

As in other continents, the first clear evidence of the systematic use of food gathered and fished from the sea or from inland waters dates from late in the Pleistocene period. Perhaps subtle population pressures were leading to adaptive radiation in subsistence. Strand-looping was among the new feeding habits; elsewhere, the radiation included shifts that led fortuitously to the crossing of the agricultural threshold. Along the coasts of many parts of Africa, especially in the zone of the cold, productive southern oceans, vast shell mounds testify to the feasibility of shellfish menus as a basis for human life. In fact the two oldest known instances of aquatic food middens are in Africa at Haua Fteah in Libya, and at Klaasies River Cave, South Africa. Both date to more than fifty thousand years ago.

Changes in the content and style of Later Stone Age industries can be well resolved in stratified rock shelters and through the use of radiocarbon dating. Variation in relation to geography and environment can be mapped. The archaeology of this period thus offers unusual opportunities for studies of the interrelationships of sociocultural, economic, and human geographic factors in a hunter-gatherer cultural system. Radiocarbon dates indicate that the first thoroughgoing microlithic industries began to be made in Africa between fifteen and twenty thousand years ago.

Stone use and hunter-gatherer ways of life were gradually replaced in Africa by iron using and the practice of farming. The process was a slow and discontinuous one that had not been completed at the time of contact with Europe. In southern Africa, explorers and colonists found Khoisan speakers such as the Bushmen hunters, who were without metals and who occupied vast tracts of land, especially dry steppe land. In central Africa, "Ba-Twa" or pygmy peoples had acquired iron from farming neighbors, but continued to live by hunting and collecting in the equatorial forests. In East Africa smaller nonagricultural pockets also survived within cultural systems dominated by farmers and pastoralists; examples are the Ndorobo of Kenya and the Hadza of Tanzania. Studies of the culture and adaptation of these peoples should not be applied in any simple way to the interpretation of prehistory; but they do provide invaluable information regarding the problems and opportunities facing hunters in Africa, along with examples of particular cultural adjustments.

• FARMING

Africa has, along with the other major continents, participated in the radical reorganization of society caused by the change from hunting-gathering subsistence to farming. The oldest archaeological evidences of food production in Africa have been found in the northeastern corner of the continent, close to the isthmus linking Africa and the Near East. Recent research has elucidated aspects of agricultural origins in the area of Anatolia, Persia, Mesopotamia, and Palestine, showing that the crop-plant and stock-animal species documented for early African sites are in fact involved in this southwest Asian nuclear area. This fact taken together with radiocarbon dates considerably less old than those for early farming sites in the Levant and Zagros lead to the conclusion that the Nile Valley and northeast Africa are to be regarded as late extensions of the nuclear area rather than integral parts of it. However, recent research in Nubia and southern Egypt has shown the existence of an extraordinarily complex system of cultures along the Nile during the Late Pleistocene and Early Holocene. We have already mentioned that some features of the evidence appear to indicate relatively high population pressures, warfare, and perhaps intensive plant-food collecting. It can certainly not be taken as proven that this part of Africa was entirely outside the nuclear area. Moreover, Africa has not been a passive recipient, and a very large number of food plants were brought into cultivation and domesticated within Africa. It is possible that this process occurred in some areas entirely independently of the spread of the idea of farming; but at present this seems unlikely.

The earliest known archaeological traces of food production in Africa are found in the long cave sequence of the Haua Fteah in Libya (shown on Map 1.1*A*), where domesticated sheep or goats first appear as part of the bone refuse in layers dated at least to 4800 B.C., and perhaps as early as 6400 B.C. In this instance, the practice of keeping stock seems to have been grafted onto a cultural regime that retained many of the traditions of the preceding Libyo-Capsian hunters, though fancy, pressure-flaked, barbed arrowheads and the use of pottery also began at much the same time. Economies combining hunting and pastoralism appear to have been well suited to conditions prevailing during the fourth and third millennia B.C. in North Africa and the Sahara. Pastoralism spread rapidly into the desert and its coastal fringes, and by about 4000 B.C. an impressive series of so-called Neolithic cultures had come into existence in this area, many of them showing strong signs of continuity with the pre-agricultural cultures of the Maghreb. At this time the Sahara, though arid, was a less extreme desert than it now is, and it was possible for nomadic peoples to support themselves by a combination of hunting, gathering, and herding, and perhaps some cultivation. The various desert Neolithic peoples thrived during the period 4500 B.C. to about 2500 B.C., when increasing desiccation seems to have diminished their numbers and successfulness. Vigorous art traditions, such as are represented for example by paintings in the rock shelters of Tassili and by engravings on the rocks of the Fezzan, have made these cultures famous.

While pastoralism spread out and developed in the great arid belt that runs across the north end of Africa, cultivation and mixed farming flourished principally in the narrow strip of lush, well-watered land that traverses the dry zone, namely the Nile Valley.

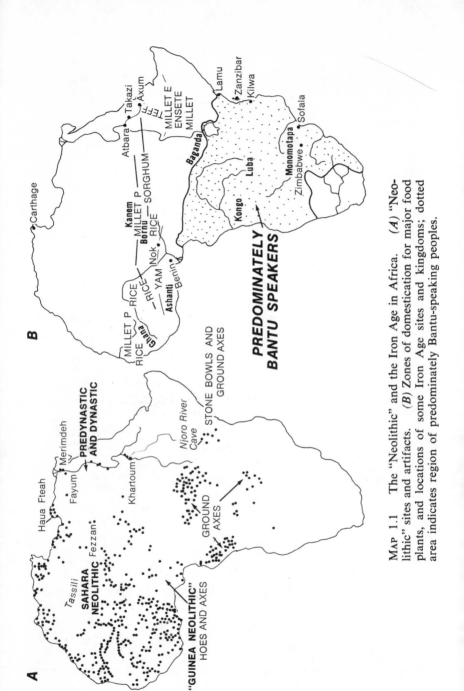

MAP 1.1   The "Neolithic" and the Iron Age in Africa.   (A) "Neolithic" sites and artifacts.   (B) Zones of domestication for major food plants, and locations of some Iron Age sites and kingdoms; dotted area indicates region of predominately Bantu-speaking peoples.

The oldest known African peasant farming villages are those of the Fayum "A" and Merimdeh in lower Egypt (4400–3800 B.C. and 4300–3700 B.C., respectively). Among other things, the people living in these places were growing wheat and barley, species which undoubtedly were introduced from the Near East. However, their material culture was in part distinct from that of adjacent areas. Since there is a gap in the known record between the dense, highly competitive early Holocene hunter-gatherers and these first known villages, it is quite possible that wheat and barley cultivation were adopted in economies that were already undergoing change in the direction of intensive collection and cultivation. In any event, technological, demographic, and political development was rapid in the Nile. A spectacular series of late prehistoric cultures known collectively as "Predynastic" flourished during the period 4000–3200 B.C. With the political unification of Upper and Lower Egypt, written records bring us to the boundary between prehistory and the history of one of the great civilizations of the ancient world.

Meanwhile, south of the Sahara, hunting-gathering economies continued to exist and differentiate themselves. There was a lag in the spread of farming which was probably caused by the unsuitability of the Mediterranean staples—wheat and barley—for cultivation under tropical conditions. Increasingly, indigenous plants were brought into cultivation around the southern fringes of the Sahara and in Ethiopia (Map 1.1*B*); while many never achieved more than local importance, others such as the yams (*Dioscorea* spp.) and the millets (*Eleusine, Pennisetum,* and *Sorghum*) became the basis for the establishment of agriculture in western Africa and central, eastern, and southern Africa. We know that these indigenous cultigens must have been domesticated in Africa, but as yet we know little about the date and manner of their entry into human exploitation. Involvement with new species of economically important domesticated animals does not appear to have occurred in sub-Saharan Africa. Because the Mediterranean species of sheep, goat, and cattle do tolerably well in the African savannahs, there was little incentive for starting the long capture and breeding process afresh, in spite of the presence of suitable ungulates in the African fauna. Because of trypanosomiasis, the tsetse fly-infested zones of Africa will not support healthy herds of Mediterranean domesticates; thus peasants in these regions traditionally subsisted without stock, except locally in West Africa where dwarf cattle developed immunity to the trypanosome parasites.

The term "Neolithic" was coined in Europe where it came to refer to cultures involving cultivation, stock rearing, villages, pottery, and ground stone. In this full sense, Neolithic cultures are conspicuous only in the prehistory of the Nile and North Africa. Even for the Sahara, the use of the term may be misleading, because the peoples largely lacked "villages," did little cultivation, and were dependent as much on hunting as herding. Further south there are in some regions traces of people who have been called Neolithic because they farmed, used pottery, and made ground stone tools, but lacked the use of iron. However, the Neolithic was not as distinctive a phase in Africa as elsewhere, and perhaps the term should not be used here. Similarly, there is no Bronze Age in sub-Saharan Africa. By the time farming was spreading into central and southern Africa, the technology of making iron was encroaching too, so that many areas shifted directly from Mesolithic tool patterns to Iron Age ones.

The practice of farming spread deeper into Africa by a number of routes: one was along the Nile, where the Khartoum Neolithic site has been known for many years. This includes the remains of domestic goat dating to about 3200 B.C. Recent research shows that by 2500 B.C. large villages, presumably dependent on agriculture, had come into being on the Atbara, a major river linking the Nile Valley with the Ethiopian highlands. As yet the story of prehistoric farming in Ethiopia is poorly known, but we can anticipate that when the area is studied there will prove to be a long and interesting record.

In humid West Africa, the addition of hoes to the material culture, together with the growing importance of pottery, and increases in the size of at least some settlements, all suggest that cultivation, perhaps principally of the yam, began to be important around 3000 B.C. However, rather little is known about the overall way of life of these peoples.

The first well-documented intrusions on the hunting-gathering economies of eastern and southeastern Africa seem to have involved pastoralism rather than cultivation. During the first millennium B.C., the highlands of Kenya and Tanzania supported peoples who had added pottery and bowls made of stone to the material culture of their Later Stone Age predecessors. They commonly buried their dead in cairns, or cremated them in crevices, as at the Njoro River site in Kenya. We know that these people were mobile pastoralists, but they may have done some cultivation as well. Pollen and sedimentological evidences suggest that at about the same time, cultivators were clearing forests in the Lake Victoria and Congo and Tanganyika basins. We know virtually nothing about these early cultivators.

• THE IRON AGE

The last segment of African prehistory began some 2500 years ago with the spread of the techniques of metal work. The ensuing period appears to have witnessed rising population densities and the restless movements of peoples and cultures. In our perception of this period of the past, we begin, dimly at first, and then more surely, to be able to identify some prehistoric cultural entities with major linguistic groupings or with the ancestors of existing peoples. For these reasons the period is sometimes known as "protohistoric."

The ancient Egyptians knew the use of copper from Predynastic times onward, and the Phoenicians also introduced copper metallurgy into such northwest African settlements as Carthage. However, the practice of metallurgy did not spread into sub-Saharan Africa until the craft of copper smelting had been joined by the much more demanding art of smelting iron. Various reasons for this are possible, one being the fact that copper ores are much rarer and more localized than the almost ubiquitous iron ores.

There are two, perhaps three, channels of contact by which iron-working techniques were communicated into Africa. In the Sudan, a literate civilization was established early in the first millennium B.C. It shared some of the cultural and artistic patterns of Dynastic Egypt, but was nonetheless distinct. Regrettably, its script and language remain undeciphered. This civilization, which is often known by the name of one of its centers, Meroë, incorporated iron technology by about 400 B.C. Vast slag heaps attest to the importance of the iron industry there. At a slightly earlier date the peoples of northwest Africa also began making iron implements. We know from engravings deep in the Sahara that depict chariots that peoples of the Mediterranean seaboard had begun to establish trade routes across the desert. It is also possible that the trade that began to grow up between the Red Sea, Persia, and the Indian Ocean coast of East Africa led to the transmission of metallurgic technology. All three lines of diffusion may have been involved independently of each other. Despite uncertainty about the initial process of the spread of iron working, we are beginning to have information on its early history. The geographic personality of Africa was again strongly expressed in the working out of cultural patterns resulting from the spread of farming and metallurgy. The major natural regions that we have seen as culturally distinctive in the Stone Age became even more so during the early Iron Age. West Africa, Ethiopia, the Congo basin, and the eastern spine of Africa from Kenya to Rhodesia from different cultural areas.

In West Africa iron was being made in fair quantities by about 400 B.C. and the oldest known smelting site is associated with the vigorous art style of Nok in northern Nigeria. The terracotta figures of this culture seem to belong within a tradition leading directly on to the famous Benin bronzes. The addition of metallurgy to farming created thriving economies which acquired trade connections across the Sahara and came thereby to be partially incorporated into the commercial life of the circum-Mediterranean world. During the last two millennia, a succession of city states and empires arose along the sudanic belt where the Sahara meets the vegetated regions of the tropics. The political and economic vicissitudes of such empires as those of Ghana, Kanem, and Bornu comprise a complex and intriguing history. Many of the peoples of the western Sudan were converted to Islam and entered the bounds of history proper through the adoption of Arabic script. West Africa acquired a strongly developed network of markets and became a mosaic of prosperous peasant societies, interspersed with various distinctive, partially urban arrangements.

Meanwhile, about two thousand years ago, new styles of pottery began to be made all over eastern Africa. These styles which are variously known as "dimple-based" or "channeled" wares appear to be associated with the beginnings of iron working. They have been found at sites scattered over a vast area extending from the Kenya Coast to Uganda, Rwanda, Burundi, the eastern Congo (Zaire), and southward to Rhodesia. So far the carbon dates for these related wares are remarkably close, and place their beginnings in the early part of the first millennium A.D., without any indication of the area of origin.

Some scholars have been tempted to try to link this archaeological pattern with a linguistic one. Most of the agriculturalists south of about 4° N. latitude in Africa speak one of a very closely related family of languages, termed *Bantu*. Similarities of structure and even vocabulary are so strong that linguists feel confident that these languages have only been differentiating for two or three thousand years at the most. Some authorities suppose that the dimple-based and channeled wares are symptomatic of a migratory expansion of early Bantu-speaking, iron-using farmers. While the possibility seems strong that the phenomena are connected, it is unclear to what extent migration actually was involved. It is likely that the new practices infiltrated rather rapidly because the initial phases of agriculture would have created demographic imbalance, and iron tools provide their possessors with economic and military advantages. It is also possible that new forms of kinship and clan-political organization were diffused at the same time, and that this may have facilitated the diffusion of Bantu languages. Modern America provides an excellent demonstration that sharing a common language system is no guarantee of derivation either from a single genetic, cultural, or linguistic stock! Probably the last two millennia of African prehistory involved a similar melting pot of genes and cultures.

Until the introduction of maize and manioc from the New World after A.D. 1500, farming in eastern and central Africa involved mixed dependence on the cultivation of millets, various root crops, and animal stock. In the tsetse-free areas, cattle were extremely important, not only for their contribution to subsistence, but also as repositories for wealth and as symbols of prestige. In the East African highlands and in the semi-arid parts of the south such non-Bantu people as the Masai and the Hottentots became purely pastoral nomads. By contrast, in much of the Congo basin and adjoining lowlands, it is difficult to rear stock, and economic patterns developed involving cultivation, fishing, and hunting, sometimes with pygmy people continuing pre-agricultural traditions so as to become part of a new symbiotic system.

Perhaps between one and two thousand years ago, food plants such as the banana and the coconut palm were introduced from the Indian Ocean, and in some areas became economically important. The idea of the xylophone, which joined the drum to become the basis for elaborate indigenous musical traditions, may also have infiltrated as a result of the Indian Ocean trade network that grew up over the past two millennia. The extent and importance of East Africa in Old World trade are known both from historic sources and from the archaeological remains of numerous trading centers along the coast, Zanzibar, Lamu, Kilwa and Sofala being among the most famous of these.

The inception of farming and the use of metals created a complex series of new social and economic trends in Africa. It is unlikely that the continent had in any sense achieved equilibrium by the time that it was forcibly incorporated by the slave trade and colonial rule into a European-dominated world commerce and politics. The first explorers found a varied patchwork of social, political, and economic conditions ranging from peasant and pastoral societies with little political integration to powerful kingdoms such as those of the Ashanti, Benin, the Kongo, the Luba, Baganda, and Monomotapa. Some of these, such as Benin, were associated with highly developed art styles; while Zimbabwe represents an extraordinary, distinctive indigenous architectural tradition developed to aggrandize the precincts of the home of a "divine" king, related to the "Monomotapa" reported in Portuguese accounts of trade and contact.

By comparison with studies of the Stone Age in Africa, the archaeology of the Iron Age has been slow to develop. It has only been during the last decade that systematic research really got underway. However, there is a rapidly growing band of specialists in this field, based both in African institutions and abroad, and already the intricacy of our information far exceeds the capacity of this chapter to do justice to the known process of development and differentiation.

In summary, then, archaeological studies in Africa yield the basis for a narrative of human activity that is more than two million years long. The story begins with small-brained, proto-human creatures possessed only of very simple equipment and organized probably in sparsely distributed hunting and foraging bands. Prehistory merges with history after the development of intricate patterns of varied economy, politics, art, and culture. The transition into the realm of history sometimes involved the rise of indigenous, literate civilizations such as those of pharaonic Egypt and Ethiopia; sometimes it came about by the incorporation of areas of Africa into wider spheres of religion, commerce, and politics.

Throughout at least the last million years, the cultural strands of African prehistory have intertwined at the borders with strands from other continents, both giving and receiving; yet there is strong continuity, and the patterns always became distinctively African.

• BIBLIOGRAPHIC ESSAY

The standard archaeological summary for the whole continent of Africa remains J. D. Clark's *The Prehistory of Africa,* published by Thames and Hudson (London), and published in a paperback edition by Praeger in 1970. The first chapters of this work provide a brief introduction to the basic techniques and goals of archaeological research, and the notes following each chapter are a valuable source of reference for specific areas and topics.

Karl W. Butzer's *Environment and Archaeology,* 2nd edition, published by Aldine in 1971, is a useful summary of paleo-environmental data relating to the changing ecological contexts of the early hominids and later Stone Age men. R. F. Flint's book *Glacial and Quaternary Geology,* published by Wiley in 1971, is also basic to an understanding of the early African environment.

The nonspecialist reader interested in a concise review of the early phases of African prehistory should consult the article by G. Ll. Isaac,

"Studies of early culture in East Africa," in *World Archaeology*, Vol. 1 (1969), No. 1. The same author provides an up-to-date review of present data (mostly faunal) relating to the subsistence of early man in his article "The diet of early man: aspects of archaeological evidence from Lower and Middle Pleistocene sites in Africa," in *World Archaeology*, Vol. 2 (1971), No. 3.

F. C. Howell's volume *Early Man*, in the Life Nature Library, published by Time-Life Books in 1965, is attractively illustrated and provides a handy nontechnical reference.

Summaries of regional prehistory are provided for South Africa by J. D. Clark's *The Prehistory of Southern Africa*, published by Pelican (London) in 1959, and C. G. Sampson's massive new volume, *The Stone Age in Southern Africa*, published by Academic Press in 1974. West African archaeology is surveyed by O. Davies in *West Africa Before the Europeans*, published by Methuen (London) in 1967. Other areas are dealt with in J. D. Clark's *Prehistoric Cultures of Northeast Angola and Their Significance in Tropical Africa*, published in two volumes in 1963 by the Museo do Dundo in Lisbon; in S. Cole's *The Prehistory of East Africa*, published by Macmillan (London) in 1963; and C. B. M. McBurney's *The Stone Age of Northern Africa*, published by Penguin (England) in 1960.

Iron Age Africa is covered by B. Davidson in *Old Africa Rediscovered*, published by Gollancz (London) in 1960, and in two recent collections of essays: *Papers in African Prehistory* by J. D. Fage and R. A. Oliver, published by Cambridge University Press in 1970, and a work edited by P. L. Shinnie, *The African Iron Age*, published by the Clarendon Press of Oxford in 1971. All of these provide useful bibliographies for further research.

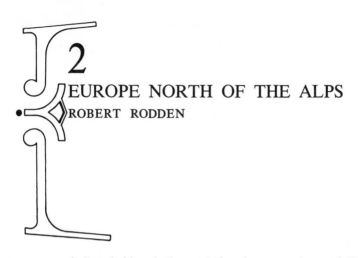

2
EUROPE NORTH OF THE ALPS
ROBERT RODDEN

A literal, historical search for the antecedents of Western civilization has been in large measure the foundation of prehistoric archaeology in Europe. Such a frankly historical bias is becoming less and less fashionable in prehistoric studies. Increasingly, the goal of contemporary research is to achieve an understanding of human behavior in prehistory. The concern of this "anthropological archaeology" is to explain the patterns of interrelation among man, his culture, and noncultural phenomena such as the natural environment; and to understand the culture-contact situations and the processes involved in cultural change. The prehistory of Europe is uniquely important to the new archaeology in that it offers, to the archaeologist willing to learn the languages, a singularly well-documented situation for exploring human behavior through approximately nine thousand years, from the end of the Ice Age to the rapid transformation of European culture under Roman influence in the first century B.C. One reason for Europe's importance is its long history of a high standard of archaeological excavation and reporting; another is the long-standing cooperation of archaeologists and scientists in prehistoric research, particularly in Scandinavia and Atlantic Europe.

• THE PERSONALITY OF EUROPE

The personality of Europe is epitomized by the biting cold wind that sweeps out of the Urals and around the streets of Cambridge,

49

England; the unending vastness of the Hungarian Plain; or the days that it may take to drive north out of an Alpine storm. In contrast to the Mediterranean basin, Europe north of the Pyrenees, Alps, and Balkan mountains is a land of great ecosystems and extensive mountain areas and plains. The continental scale of the major environmental features—relief, soils, climate, and native plant and animal communities—allows for the comparative analysis of different exploitative strategies in comparable ecological settings; the archaeologist can also examine adaptations to environments that are fundamentally similar but vary in one or another specific respect.

In terms of relief, the tectonically stable and horizontally bedded rocks of much of northern Europe and European Russia (that is, Russia west of the Urals and north of the Caucasus) delineate one major base-line: the lowlying northern European plains and tablelands. Beyond them to the north and west lie the Scandinavian mountains and the Scottish, Welsh, and Irish highlands, all remnants of ancient Caledonian mountain building, and the last retreats of the British-Scandinavian Late Glacial icecap. South of the northern European plains and tablelands and at the heart of central and western Europe lies a core of upland blocks ranging from the Massif Central on the west to the Bohemian highlands on the east. South and east of these are the products of the Alpine phase of mountain building: the Pyrenees; the Western, Eastern, and Illyrian Alps; and the Carpathians.

The vegetation can be divided into essentially latitudinal zones—temperate deciduous forest, northern coniferous forest, and circumpolar tundra—which to some extent cut across relief boundaries. In historic times most of the mid-latitudes of Europe have been covered with deciduous forest. Where suitable climatic conditions occur south of this zone, as in parts of the Balkans and along the Atlantic coast of the Iberian peninsula, deciduous forest may also be found. Important trees in the deciduous woodland are oak, elm, lime, alder, and beech; all are broad-leaved varieties which have their period of growth in summer and shed their leaves in autumn. The northern coniferous forest comprises a broad belt of pine, spruce, and silver fir which, along with birch and willow, cover much of Scandinavia, Finland, and most of European Russia north of the limits of deciduous forest. The adaptation here is to moist, cold climatic conditions. North of the coniferous forest zone, in areas dominated by arctic or subarctic climates, is a belt of circumpolar tundra. Map 2.1 shows the vegetation zones as well as the locations of some major archaeological sites that pertain to the sections that follow.

Other geographical common denominators can be defined that relate either to economy or to technology: for example, the well-drained loess soils that cover much of temperate Europe and that were important for the spread of agriculture; and the absence of copper and tin ores on the northern European plain, despite which a flourishing bronze industry developed in southern Scandinavia and northern Germany.

• POST-PLEISTOCENE ENVIRONMENTAL CHANGE AND HUNTER-FISHER ADAPTATIONS

The large-scale relief and latitudinal zonation of vegetation in Europe dictated that environmental responses to the climatic changes of the terminal Pleistocene and early Holocene be similar over wide areas and comparatively straightforward in their manifestations. The principal factor in these changes was temperature. With the rise in temperature in the final phases of the Pleistocene and early post-Pleistocene, and the retreat in stages of the northern European icecap across northern Europe to the Scandinavian and British highlands, there were clearly documented shifts northward of the various major ecological zones and clearly traceable changes in the land's relationship to the sea. Here is a circumstance as close to ideal as the archaeologist is likely to find for studying man's adaptations in the face of marked ecological change. Fortunately, there has been a long-standing interest in the problems of Late Pleistocene and post-Pleistocene climatic and environmental change in northwestern Europe, and our knowledge of the extent of glacier ice at different times in its final retreat, of former sea levels and coastlines, and of regional vegetational histories as documented by pollen analysis, is possibly more complete than for any other area of comparable size in the world.

Two major questions have been asked regarding the history of

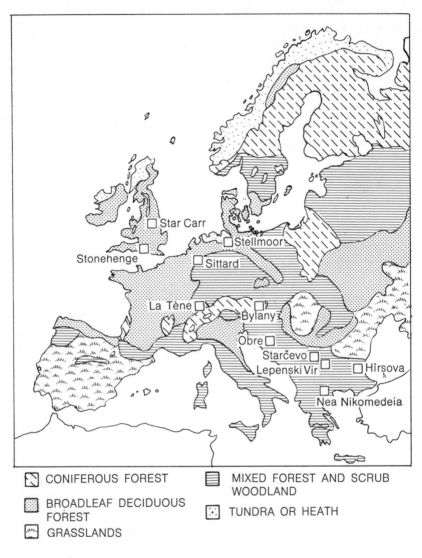

MAP 2.1   Vegetation areas and selected sites in Europe.

hunter-fisher adaptations in Late Glacial and early post-Glacial Europe. The first concerns the fate of the Upper Paleolithic reindeer- and mammoth-hunters who occupied the ice-free areas of Europe at the close of the Pleistocene. The second concerns the development of the specialized inland and coastal varieties of the northern Mesolithic.

To answer both questions we need a precise understanding of (1) the nature of the climatic, vegetational, and faunal changes involved, and (2) the developing patterns of subsistence economy, tool kits, settlement location, and population density. The available evidence suggests that a complex series of relationships is involved, of which irregular, violent oscillations between warmer and colder conditions constitute one set of factors, and various "lag" phenomena another.

The time span in question is the 11,000 years between 14,000 B.C., an approximate date for the beginnings of the protracted glacier retreat of the early Late Würm, and 3000 B.C., the end of the post-Pleistocene climatic optimum when conditions in Europe were both warmer and moister than those existing at the present time. The transformations in ecological setting that took place during this eleven-thousand-year interval in northern Europe can be briefly summarized by referring to the stages in the development of vegetation; pollen analysis has demonstrated that such development was more or less comparable, if not precisely parallel, throughout the area.

Generally, in the Late Würm (14,000–8300 B.C.) arctic climatic conditions prevailed and open tundra covered the north European plain and east European steppe; in central and southwestern Europe there was either forest-tundra or birch and pine woodland. Two brief warm intervals occurred in the Late Würm during which the southern woodland belts moved northward. The first of these warm interludes is known as the Bölling and dates to between about 11,500 and 10,500 B.C. During the second oscillation, called the Allerød and dated to between 10,000 and 8800 B.C., open woodlands spread over much of ice-free Europe and the tundra was confined to small areas marginal to the ice-sheets. While the precise relationship between these changes and the resident fauna (including reindeer, mammoth, woolly rhinoceros, musk ox, giant elk, bison, and horse) is not clear, it is a fact that by the end of the Allerød only the more versatile reindeer survived. Because of low sea levels and limited deglaciation in the Late Glacial, Britain was still connected to the continent by the northern European plain across what is now the English Channel and the southern portion of the North Sea; the Scandinavian icecap shut off the open sea from the Baltic, where there was an ice-dammed freshwater lake.

With the early post-Glacial rise in temperature the changes in environment became more drastic. In the earliest post-Glacial phase, known as the pre-Boreal and dating to between 8300 and possibly 7500 B.C., the subarctic tundra/parkland of the final episode of the Late Glacial was in large part replaced by birch woodland. The birch was a "pioneer" species that rapidly colonized the tundra and the barren lands left free by the retreat of the ice. In the long run the disappearance of the open herbaceous tundra from most of Europe forced the final local extinction and northward migration of the herds of reindeer that depended on it. The rapid expansion of open woodland in the pre-Boreal brought with it solitary browsing game animals, such as red and roe deer, elk and aurochs, and the foraging wild boar. Equally important to the changes in the biome were the alterations in coastlines, which affected the amount and kind of land available for human settlement. The retreat of the ice from the western Baltic in the pre-Boreal and the accompanying rise in sea level turned the Late Glacial Baltic ice-dammed lake into an inland salt-water sea. Britain still remained tied to the continent by the as yet unflooded English Channel and the southern portion of the North Sea. The climate of the succeeding Boreal period (7500 B.C.? to about 5600 B.C.) was warmer and drier than that of the pre-Boreal. The accompanying changes in vegetation in northern Europe only partly document these climatic changes. More important is that the "pioneer" species of the pre-Boreal open woodland gradually succumbed to more tenacious and tolerant "climax" species. The first of these to migrate into the area was hazel, the appearance of which in the fossil pollen record defines the Boreal period. The continuing rise in sea level cut Britain off from continental Europe at this time. In the western Baltic, the rebound of land—a delayed response to the removal of the weight of glacial ice—outpaced the rise in sea level and converted the inland sea once more into a vast lake. A further amelioration of climate and a worldwide rise in sea level, marking the climatic optimum, brought the sea back into the Baltic at higher levels than those existing at the present time. Not only in the Baltic, but also in the Low Countries, many areas were flooded and coastlines were greatly altered. In the Atlantic period (5500–3000 B.C.) in northwest Europe, the climax species of the deciduous forest (elm, lime, and oak) moved in; this had a detrimental effect on such game animals as the aurochs and red deer, which had been able to browse more successfully on the undergrowth of the more open woodland that was now replaced. Inland lakes and marshes became filled with vegetation; they were converted into raised bogs, killing off fish and waterfowl.

Chart 2.1 summarizes the developments between 14,000 and 3000 B.C. Of all these changes in environment, those which accompanied the Late Glacial/pre-Boreal transition and the Boreal/Atlantic transition seem to have had the greatest effect on the history of hunter-gatherer patterns on the northern European plain.

The nature and extent of the modifications in life-way that accompanied the Late Glacial/pre-Boreal transition, and which were prompted by the disappearance of reindeer (probably early in the pre-Boreal), can be appreciated by comparing the remains from the north German site of Stellmoor, which dates to the final cold oscillation of the Late Glacial, with those from the late pre-Boreal site of Star Carr in northeastern England. The Stellmoor site is situated in one of the tunnel valleys left by the retreating glacial ice on the northern European plain. It was a natural trap for herds of reindeer close to what must have been the northern limit of their summer migration. Reindeer, in fact, were by far the most important animal hunted. The rarity of shed reindeer antler and the predominance of bones of calves one and two summers in age in the Stellmoor fauna argue strongly for its having been a summer camp; the quantity of animal bone suggests that the inhabitants may have returned annually to the site for as long as a generation. One cannot mention the reindeer hunters of Stellmoor without noting the seven-foot-high pole surmounted by a fine head (skull with antlers) of an old buck that was found at the site, and the

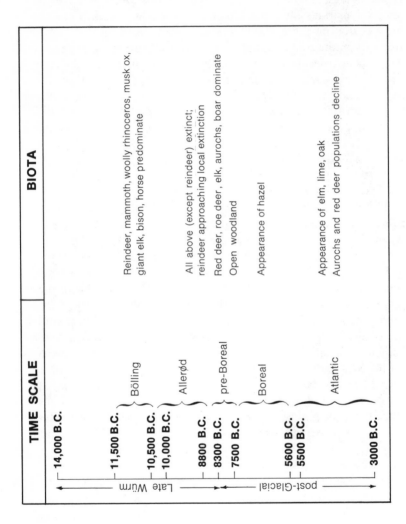

TIME SCALE		BIOTA
14,000 B.C.		
11,500 B.C.	Bölling	Reindeer, mammoth, woolly rhinoceros, musk ox, giant elk, bison, horse predominate
10,500 B.C.	Allerød	
10,000 B.C.		All above (except reindeer) extinct; reindeer approaching local extinction
8800 B.C.	pre-Boreal	Red deer, roe deer, elk, aurochs, boar dominate
8300 B.C.		Open woodland
7500 B.C.	Boreal	Appearance of hazel
5600 B.C.		
5500 B.C.	Atlantic	Appearance of elm, lime, oak
		Aurochs and red deer populations decline
3000 B.C.		

Late Würm — post-Glacial

CHART 2.1   Major climatological time periods and associated biota.

thirty bodies of sacrificial reindeer does, weighted down with stones, that were deposited in the now-vanished lake adjacent to the site. Star Carr, too, was a temporary encampment. Like Stellmoor, Star Carr appears to have been abandoned and reoccupied a number of times (during mid-winter and spring rather than during summer); however, the Star Carr camping place was much smaller in total area than Stellmoor. The Star Carr settlement was situated on a gravel promontory in an early post-Glacial lake (there was actually a rough platform of birch brushwood on the lakeward half of the site), with immediate access to the open-water lake, its bordering reed swamps, and the dense birch woods behind the site. The importance of the site's accessibility to these various micro-environments is reflected in the wide-spectrum utilization of their resources. Unlike Stellmoor, a variety of big game animals were important in Star Carr's food quest: red deer, aurochs, elk, roe deer, and boar. Significantly, despite the lakeside situation of the camp and the discovery of a paddle, as well as numerous barbed spearpoints of antler which elsewhere are associated with pike fishing, the evidence for the hunting of waterbirds is minimal and there is no direct evidence that fishing had been carried on at all.

Figures 2.1*A–B* and 2.2*A* show some cultural aspects of Stellmoor and Star Carr.

The Star Carr pattern appears to be typical of the early adaptations of Mesolithic groups to the pre-Boreal and Boreal inland environments of the northern European plain. It has been argued that this pattern represents the dramatic and sudden readjustment of hunters and gatherers to a resource crisis brought about by the disappearance of the reindeer. Undoubtedly, a broadening of the food resource base and the development of new hunting techniques appropriate to the pursuit of individual animals were crucial factors in the readjustment process. But did these innovations follow environmental changes or were they inherent in the "pre-adaptive" aspects of northern European plain culture in the late Upper Paleolithic? Some of the similarities and differences between the Upper Paleolithic of the northern European plain, as represented by Stellmoor (Ahrensburgian culture), and the early Mesolithic, as represented by Star Carr (Proto-Maglemosian and Maglemosian), have already been noted. In order to understand the pro-

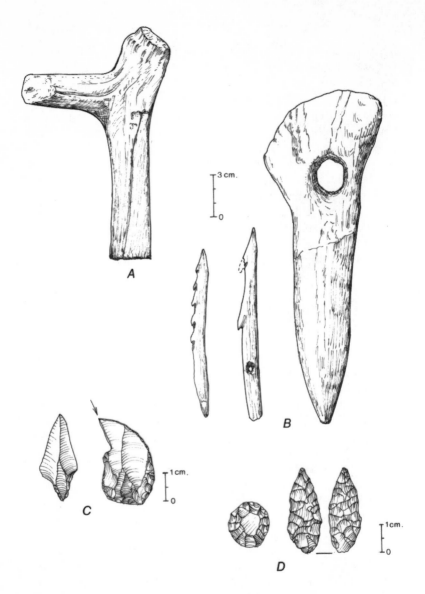

FIGURE 2.1   Artifacts of the post-Pleistocene.   *(A)* Antler club from Stellmoor.   *(B)* Mattock head and spearpoints from Star Carr. *(C)* Magdalenian stone implements.   *(D)* Sauveterrian-Tardenoisian tools.

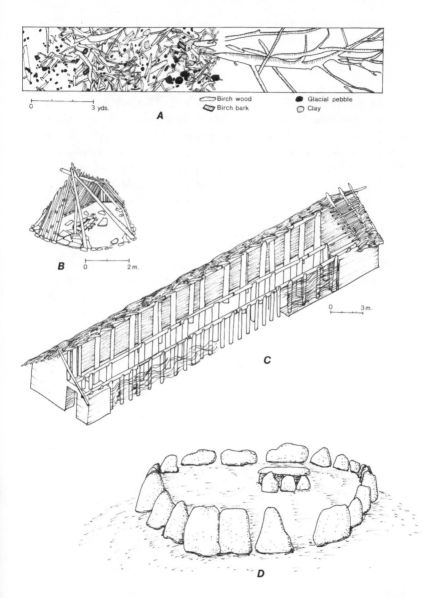

FIGURE 2.2   Architectural phenomena from northern Europe.   *(A)*
Star Carr.   *(B)* Lepenski Vir.   *(C)* Bylany.   *(D)* Danish megalith.

cesses of the changes, the following points may also be noted: The Ahrensburgian is not exclusively a reindeer-hunting culture. Contemporary with Stellmoor are cave sites with a similar tool kit, and a fauna comprising both forest and tundra animals. In terms of innovations in hunting techniques, success in solitary game hunting depended indisputably upon the bow and arrow. As a new invention, however, the bow and arrow had first made its appearance on the northern European plain with the Ahrensburgian reindeer hunters. With the new life-way, it replaces the harpoon as an object of elaboration and of the craftsman's pride. Fowling and pike fishing are known from the Ahrensburgian (from Stellmoor); while apparently of little importance to pre-Boreal hunters and gatherers, both activities were an integral part of the food quest in the Boreal, as indicated by abundant bird and fish remains at Maglemosian sites.

Population density appears to have been profoundly affected by the disappearance of the reindeer. In those parts of the northern European plain that are exceptionally well known archaeologically, the number of pre-Boreal sites is significantly lower than either that from the earlier Late Glacial or from the succeeding Boreal. The implication is that in the short term, the disappearance of the traditionally hunted reindeer constituted a game crisis that was met either by emigration, famine, or some other mechanism of population reduction. Changes in the size of living groups do not seem to have been appreciable. Sites such as Star Carr are neither larger nor smaller than the majority of reindeer-hunting encampments. There are exceptions like Stellmoor; however, it is possible that in the annual cycle of group activities these exceptions represent a short-term joining together of forces for a reindeer *battue* or herd hunt. In the long term—in the Boreal—there is an upswing in population that probably approaches the carrying capacity of the land and reflects the successful adjustment by Maglemosian groups to the land's full potential.

With the onset of Atlantic climatic conditions, Mesolithic man on the northern European plain faced another crisis of a very different sort. Not one but a combination of changes was involved; the concerted effect was to concentrate settlement on the coasts and to make maritime and riverine fishing, and the hunting of sea mammals, important to the economy. At the end of the Boreal, elk and aurochs are already becoming rare in the faunal assemblages from Maglemosian sites in Denmark, reflecting their diminishing numbers in the woodland as it is replaced by the oak-mixed forest. In these same assemblages there is an increase in the importance of waterfowl, fish, and wild fruits and berries. But with the filling in of lakes and the growth of bogs in Atlantic times, this resource, too, disappears. When one considers that the contemporary rise in sea level further reduced the territory available for inland hunting and extended the length of coastlines, it is not surprising that adjustments increasingly emphasized the sea as an important resource. This transition is best documented from the west Baltic area, where the coastal facies in settlement pattern and economy plays a significant and important role in the subsequent prehistoric development of the area.

Elsewhere in temperate Europe, the amelioration of climate in the early post-Glacial does not appear to have had the pronounced effect upon environments and hunter-gatherer adjustments that it did in the northern European lowlands; rather, it is the spread of the oak-mixed forest in Atlantic times that appears to have been the single environmental factor most disruptive to the hunting and gathering existence in many areas. In many inland areas there is a discernible continuity in hunting pattern that begins with Late Glacial forest-adapted Magdalenian hunters and continues, with only minor modifications, down to the climatic optimum. On the Atlantic coast of northern Spain, an exploitative pattern involving both the hunting of woodland species and the collecting of marine shellfish begins in the Magdalenian and continues, possibly with interruptions, through the climatic optimum.

It is not surprising that in the long interval between approximately 10,000 B.C. and 3000 B.C. significant changes should have occurred in tool-making traditions. In many areas the Upper Paleolithic and derivative technologies (Magdalenian/Azilian, Tjongerian, Creswellian, and so forth) appear to give way in the eighth millennium B.C. to a Sauveterrian-Tardenoisian tradition. "Penknife" points, thumbnail scrapers, and burins are characteristic of the former; geometric microlithic points and the notch-and-microburin technique, of the latter (Figure 2.1C–D). These cultural changes appear to be largely independent of economy and ecological setting. The archaeological reality of the matter is that the evidence from the crucial early phases of the post-Glacial period remains comparatively meagre and poorly understood.

• THE EARLY FARMING CULTURES
AND THEIR RELATIONSHIPS

It has been suggested that the oak-mixed forest which gradually spread over temperate Europe in Atlantic times established such an unfavorable environment for the game and other resources traditionally exploited by Mesolithic man that he moved toward the coast and added coastal hunting, fishing, and collecting to his subsistence pattern. Corollary with this hypothesis are two important points: first, that in this process great areas of inland Europe became virtually depopulated; and second, that the more permanent and more populous coastal settlements made possible by the great potential wealth and year-round availability of marine resources somewhat anticipated the residential stability that accompanied the spread of farming. The hypothesis is attractive as an explanation of the apparent scarcity of evidence for Mesolithic occupation in many inland areas between about 5500 B.C. and the explosive spread of Danubian "Bandkeramik" farming culture between 4400 and 4000 B.C. Before examining the spread of the Bandkeramik peasant farmers, it is necessary first to consider their progenitors, the first farming groups in temperate Europe: the farming groups of southeastern Europe that appear in the archaeological record in the sixth millennium B.C.

The early farming cultures of the northern Balkan peninsula and the middle and lower reaches of the Danube (present-day Bulgaria, Yugoslavia, Rumania, and southeastern Hungary) are the earliest in temperate Europe. Their material cultures contain many features that suggest that they represent an extension—into a new area and new environments—of a village-farming way of life which at a slightly earlier time is found on the coasts of the northern Aegean and in western Anatolia. From the beginning, these cultures are "fully formed" Neolithic in the sense that cereal cultivation and animal husbandry, ground and polished stone tools, and pottery were all present. Like their counterparts in the northern Aegean, clay stamp-seals and figurines, and pottery tables or altars are present on many sites. The question that archaeologists are asking today is whether the fully formed Neolithic character of these first peasant farming communities is the product of immigration, massive acculturation, independent discovery, or some combination of the three.

While provincial traits in material culture do exist, the precise correspondences throughout the area in figurines, stamp-seals, the use of bone spoons, and the chipped-stone tool kit are more striking. Even some pottery forms and decorations are replicated from region to region. Such a measure of unity cannot be considered a feature of the later prehistoric archaeology of the Balkans; it suggests that in the *earliest* Neolithic we are dealing with a fairly close-knit group of communities throughout which changes in taste and values, and technological, economic, and social innovations, operated with an overall effect. An example of such an overall trend is the increase in importance through time and from southeast to northwest of fine painted ware in the pottery assemblages. Culturally speaking, the northern Balkan Early Neolithic farmers were looking toward the southeast, a direction that could be considered characteristic of an immigrant's world-view.

In the face of the extremely sparse data on subsistence and settlement it is difficult to weigh the relative importance of environmental and cultural factors in delineating significant regional differences in these aspects of the earliest farming culture in southeastern Europe. Possibly the most clear-cut difference is the virtual absence of *tell,* or mound, sites on the southern part of the Hungarian plain north of Belgrade, an important area of early settlement. Even here one must be wary of imputing great significance to a trait, the presence of which may indicate nothing more than the amount of mud used in domestic building and the local availability of timber. Excepting the thick accumulations of disintegrated mud walling that characterize *tell* sites, *tell* and non-mounded settlements appear to be broadly similar. Settlements rarely exceeded 200 meters in maximum dimension and probably the largest villages numbered no more than 300–400 individuals. At *tell* sites, such as those found on the central Bulgarian plain, the settlement plans of which have been masterfully recovered by Bulgarian archaeologists, closely spaced, detached, single-room dwellings were the norm. In general, alluvial plains, valley bottoms, or the immediately adjacent hills were the preferred location for settlements. Sheep and goat and wheat and barley were mainstays to the economy, but on later sites in the northern part of the area, cattle keeping and hunting assume local importance. These northern variations in subsistence economy are of great interest. Complementing the high proportion of cattle in the domestic faunas of Yugoslav Starčevo sites (Obre I and Lepenski Vir III), Hungarian Körös culture sites, and Rumanian Criş culture sites, is morphological evidence that cattle were newly and locally domesticated from wild aurochs in at least the former two provinces of the temperate southeastern European Early Neolithic. The increased importance of cattle at the expense of sheep and goats among these groups may be partly explained by the hypothesis that in the new environment sheep and goat breeding was not sufficient both to maintain herd size and to supply the people's meat requirements. Hunting in these communities may have served the same end as the keeping of cattle—that of maintaining the level of meat resources. The importance of hunting is of further interest in connection with the scarcity of inland fish and game, the persistence of local Mesolithic hunters and gatherers, and the role of these hunters and gatherers in the spread of the Neolithic.

Paleobotanical investigations from a part of the Hungarian plain immediately adjacent to the periphery of these primary European farming settlements suggest that unlike many other parts of central, northern, and northwestern Europe, the Hungarian plain in Atlantic times maintained both open country and broadleaved woodland, the latter along rivers and on hillsides.

The discovery at the Lepenski Vir site, situated in the ecologically diverse Iron Gate gorge of the Danube where the river cuts through the Carpathian mountains, of two very substantial occupations (Lepenski Vir I and II) which antedated the Early Neolithic settlement and which relied completely upon hunting and fishing, disproves the thesis that local hunting and fishing Mesolithic populations did not exist. Furthermore, the discovery in the first stratum alone of 104 houses assignable to five successive building phases leaves little doubt that in exceptional environmental circumstances, such as those found at Lepenski Vir, residential stability was both possible and actual at inland Mesolithic sites. These houses (Figure 2.2*B*) are closely spaced, trapezoidal, and facing the Danube. They have rock-hard plaster floors colored red or white and a centrally positioned rectangular hearth. A unique series of remarkable boulder-sculptures comes from the site, many standing in front or behind the hearths of the houses. The most striking of these sculptures (Figure 2.3*A*) are life-size heads with fish-like features; these have a certain monumental quality. However, in terms of our own aesthetic, they are melancholy and lacking in vitality. Other Mesolithic sites with microlithic tool kits broadly comparable to those from Lepenski Vir I and II are known from the northern Balkans. Like Lepenski Vir, most have very little in common with the earliest Neolithic assemblages. This suggests that the acculturation of these Mesolithic groups played little part in the important transformations that Early Neolithic economy and society underwent in this area.

This early adjustment of southeastern European farming groups to temperate woodland environments is followed by the colonization of what is essentially the rest of temperate Europe by farming communities belonging to the "linear pottery" phase of Danubian Bandkeramik culture. In the 400 years between approximately 4400 B.C. and 4000 B.C., these groups appear on the well-drained loess soils everywhere from southern Holland to the eastern slopes of the Carpathians, and from the Alpine foreland to northern Germany and Poland. The radiocarbon and comparative dating evidence leave little doubt that most regions were settled earlier rather than later in the culture's 400–500 years duration. Throughout this great area there is a standardization in economy, tool kit, pottery, house, and settlement form unparalleled in the later prehistoric record. Linear Bandkeramik groups lived by agriculture and husbandry. Cattle was the most important domesticated animal to most communities. Wild animal bones rarely amount to more than 10 percent of the faunal assemblages, except in Rumania. Villages cover enormous areas (over 60,000 square meters have been excavated at the Czechoslovakian site of Bylany), lie thick on the ground, and comprise heavy, timber-framed dwellings 5–7

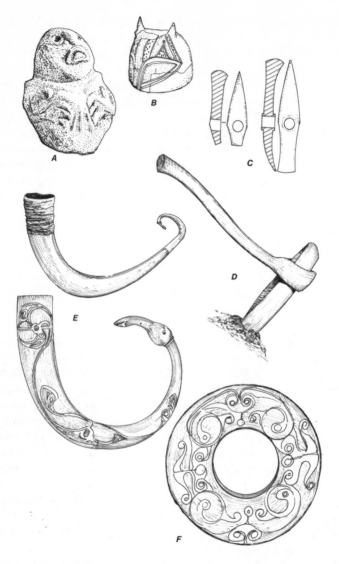

FIGURE 2.3   Artifacts of Mesolithic, Neolithic, and Iron Age Europe.   *(A)* Sculpture from Lepenski Vir.   *(B)* Cat-face lid from Vinča.   *(C)* Copper axes from southeastern Europe.   *(D)* Stone axe.   *(E)* Early La Tène grave goods.   *(F)* Late La Tène motif.

meters wide and measuring up to 45 meters in length. (See Figure 2.2*C*.)

Archaeologists have long assumed that colonization was the process at work in the rapid spread of Bandkeramik culture, prompted by a deserted Europe and a shifting agriculture based upon slash-and-burn cultivation. By ethnographic analogy it was argued that extended families numbering 20–25 individuals occupied each of the long-houses, of which (as demonstrated by excavation) there were perhaps 10–20 or even more in each village. These villages were seen as impermanent settlements: such large population units would rapidly have exhausted local soils and depleted the other resources of the Atlantic oak-mixed forest; once this happened they would move on.

There are difficulties and inconsistencies in such a model; because such problems demonstrate the inevitable vagaries of archaeological interpretation and the fleeting usefulness of models in the face of new evidence, it is worthwhile to consider this model. The earliest phase of linear Bandkeramik development occurs on the northwestern periphery of the southeastern European Neolithic; thus it is generally presumed that linear Bandkeramik groups are in some way descendants of the earlier cultures. A southeastern orientation, and possibly origin, for the Bandkeramik pattern is suggested in the affiliations that the earliest linear Bandkeramik pottery shows with the Körös and Starčevo facies of the Balkan Early Neolithic, in the close similarity in economies (the scarcity of wild animals in the faunal assemblages from Bandkeramik sites can be accounted for by the hypothesis that they moved into a Europe already scarce in game), and in the preference of early Bandkeramik peoples for ornaments of *Spondylus* shell from the Aegean or northern Adriatic. Inconsistent with this model are the impermanent character of Bandkeramik settlements (the southeastern European *tell* settlements are generally considered to be permanent villages) and the differences in social organization implied by large versus small house types.

New evidence from Bylany and from the important Dutch site of Sittard call into question the size and character of Bandkeramik occupation by suggesting that the living village was much smaller and more permanent than the building and settlement plans might lead one to assume. The first indications came from Sittard where the fossil pollen record from a nearby bog indicated that that settlement's impact upon the local Atlantic forest was minimal in comparison with that of later Neolithic occupations. Careful study of the house plans revealed that the standard long-house (known as the Geleen-type) regularly was divided into three parts, each with its own function: a northwestern part, with many variably placed posts, that probably served as a cattle byre or stable; a less cluttered central living area, of a size convenient for a nuclear family but not for an extended one; and a southeastern part, which had a plastered outside wall and an arrangement of posts suggestive of a granary. The average diameter of the posts used in the Sittard buildings was 40–50 centimeters. There can be little doubt that these buildings were meant to last, and that as a settlement, Sittard was fairly permanent. At Bylany, where after twelve years of work, 108 houses have been uncovered, stratigraphic evidence, archaeomagnetic dating of the pottery, and a quantitative study of the contents of more than 1000 associated pits have suggested that 21 occupation phases are represented at the site, each with perhaps only 7 or 8 houses. For one of the best-known occupations, the red phase, it has been argued that the number of nuclear families per house varied from 1 to 4, and that the village numbered some 40–50 adults and 150 children. Each occupation is thought to have lasted between 12 and 15 years, after which the group would successively settle at other sites in the immediate vicinity, to return 60 years later after the forest had been regenerated. Such a reconstruction of the Bandkeramik life-way, of small, fairly permanent villages comprised of nuclear families variously grouped, and of a long-term cyclical agriculture, is not inconsistent with the nature and character of some of the early southeastern European farming settlements, for example Nea Nikomedeia in northern Greece. But it leaves unexplained the explosive nature of the spread of Bandkeramik culture which the "big picture" derived from archaeology suggests.

• EXPANSION AND DIVERSIFICATION

In the later phases of linear Bandkeramik development, regional differentiation in pottery form and decoration is discernible. In the

1000–1500 years succeeding 4000 B.C.—with population increase and the spread of farming economy into the Alps, southern Russian steppe, and maritime provinces of northwestern Europe— regionalization becomes more marked. This is particularly evident in the pottery assemblages, whose varying characteristics have defined the different regional cultures and traditions. In southeastern Europe there are the roughly contemporaneous Vinča culture (Figure 2.3*B*) centered on the Vardar-Morava drainages of Serbia and Yugoslav Macedonia, the Gumelnitsa/Salcutsa complex of the lower Danube basin and Bulgaria, and the Tiszapolgár and Bodrogkeresztúr cultures of Transylvania and Hungary. Bubanj Hum, Cernavoda/Ezero, and Baden-Pecél are names given to later cultures in these same areas. For the south Russian steppe, the succession pre-Cucuteni-Cucuteni-Tripolje has been defined. In the former linear Bandkeramik area, evolved Danubian stroke-ornamented pottery cultures are found in the central area, while in the west there is the Rössen culture. These in turn give way to various regional expressions of the Funnel-Beaker culture (TRB) and Michelsberg culture. The Neolithic settlement of the Alpine foreland and Alps proper is documented in the histories of the Rössen and stroke-ornamented pottery cultures already mentioned, in the Aichbühl culture, and later in the Cortaillod, Egolzwil, and Pfyn cultures of Switzerland, the Schussenried culture of south Germany, and the Mondsee culture of Austria. On the northern European plain, the Ertebølle culture is found on the coast, and the Funnel-Beaker culture inland. The Chassey cultural tradition dominates France and the Early/Middle Neolithic bowl culture, the British Isles.

Prehistorians working in each of these areas have concentrated on defining the spatial and temporal dimensions of these and innumerable other cultural entities. They have also ardently debated questions of origins, internal development, and external relations, an enterprise that would be unproductive for us to pursue. Rather, we may focus on the phenomenon of regional and subregional divergence that is suggested for most areas during this period, and speculate on the causes underlying the alterations and transformations in social alignments that such differentiation reflects. Limitations of space allow us to consider this only with reference to several selected examples.

In the case of southeastern Europe, the likelihood must be considered that the regional and subregional differences in pottery, which serve to define the archaeological cultures, reflect the emergence of a new economic system in which craft specialization and local centers of production play important roles. The southeastern European cultures mentioned above belong to the first metal-using communities of Europe. The early dating of these cultures relative to the Early Bronze Age cultures of the Aegean leaves little doubt that copper metallurgy (Figure 2.3C) was independently invented; and the comparative uninventiveness of the metallurgical tradition, once established, argues that it was in the hands of a closed craft community. That it evolved essentially in isolation over a considerable period of time may be seen as a manifestation of the essentially regional scale of the contemporary trade networks. Workshops have actually been found. At Chotnica in Bulgaria a workshop—complete with specialized tools—of a craftsman who produced bone figurines of a type popular in the area was uncovered. A *Spondylus* shell workshop has been reported from the site of Hîrşova, also in Bulgaria. In Rumania a flint workshop has been claimed from the site of Căscioarele. The discovery of large stores of pottery vessels, as well as evidence that complex and carefully controlled manufacturing techniques were required for the diagnostic, graphite-decorated pottery of the Gumelnitsa culture, makes it highly probable that the pottery too was in the hands of craft specialists and local entrepreneurs.

Regionalization in those areas of temperate Europe that were newly settled by farming groups appears to have been mostly a reflection of "digging in" to new and different habitats. In the realm of subsistence economics, regional and subregional differences that sometimes involve highly specialized adaptations have been worked out for the Alps and Baltic areas; but the question of how, or if, economic and ecological isolation affected cultural divergence has not yet been attacked. Information that is relevant to these questions is available for the British Isles. As in the other areas just mentioned, local Mesolithic groups (in this case Larnian and Obanian coastal settlements along the Irish Sea) may have been the first to adopt elements of Neolithic culture and economy. However, the first stable Neolithic farming system to develop in the British Isles, which may date as early as 3800–3700 B.C. in Ireland, appears culturally to have owed little to native Mesolithic populations, and rather more to regular contacts with contemporary groups on the continent. Like them (but unlike the earlier linear Bandkeramik farmers), the groups in Britain cleared much woodland for cultivation and grazing, mainly of cattle; this is decisively represented in pollen diagrams. The existence of a primarily pastoralist Highland subculture and of a primarily agriculturalist Lowland subculture is implied in the dearth of milling equipment, grain impressions in pottery, and storage pits at sites in the highland zone. Such differences in economy undoubtedly encouraged subregional solidarity, but there is no question of complete isolation. A flourishing trade in stone axe-blades (Figure 2.3*D*) grew up between factories in North Wales and the Lake District—both in the highland zone—and lowland southern England. The two areas share basic cultural traits as well, but in a manner that suggests that in both areas it is the local combination of elements, such as that found on the North Wiltshire chalk downs, that is unique and important. This is as true of the pottery as it is of another defining feature of the British Neolithic: its impressive burial monuments and "henges."

• MEGALITHS: EUROPE'S FIRST
ARCHITECTURAL EXPERIENCE

Perhaps none of the prehistoric monuments of Europe excite the imagination so much as Stonehenge and the related megalithic (great stone) "temples" and tombs (see Figure 2.2*D*). They stand out against the landscape because of the gigantic size of the stones used in their construction. The siting, mathematical planning, and public-works scale of these undertakings, and the balance of mass and space evident in many structures, are in the tradition of a monumental if not "grand" architecture. There is common agreement that the earliest expression of the tradition was in the "chambered" tombs, which are much more numerous and widespread than the nonchambered megalithic monuments: single standing stones (menhirs), alignments (for example, Carnac in northwestern France), and "henges" (for example, Stonehenge and Avebury in southern England). Because of the rarity with which undisturbed primary deposits are found in these tombs, the question of the date of their construction, and therefore of the origins of megalithic building in Europe, has long vexed archaeologists. Most archaeologists thought in terms of an ultimate eastern Mediterranean, pre-Mycenaean origin. The requisite technical and organizational skills, and the custom of collective inhumation burial, were already in existence there from around 2500 B.C. (a date based upon established links between Minoan Crete and historically dated Egypt). There were also the impressive similarities in plan and construction between one important class of western European chambered tombs—the passage graves of Iberia, France, northern Britain, and Ireland—and the Mycenaean *tholos* tombs of mainland Greece, which bespoke a cousin-like relationship.

The picture has been radically altered with the application of radiocarbon dating to the problem; and the theories that explained the relationship in terms of a colonist or diffusion spread of megalithic tombery from the eastern Mediterranean to Spain and Portugal, and then to maritime western Europe, have become less than tenable. There are radiocarbon age determinations that suggest that megaliths were being built in Scandinavia as early as 2900 B.C. Charcoal from underneath the mound of a satellite grave to an Irish passage grave gave dates of 2925 ± 150 B.C. and 2845 ± 185 B.C. Passage graves in Brittany, northwestern France, have been dated to as early as 3200–3000 B.C. In all these areas other types of chamber tombs (gallery graves, transepted chamber tombs under long barrows and long cairns) are found with equally early dates. For the Iberian passage graves there is a date of 2300 ± 60 B.C. from Praia das Macas in Portugal. These dates in radiocarbon years, if calibrated with calendrical years using the bristlecone pine tree-ring chronology of Hans Suess, would fall well inside the fourth millennium B.C.: more than 500 years before the pyramids, 2000 years before the Minoan tombs, and 2500 years before the Mycenaean parallels. By the same chronology, Stonehenge, built in three main periods spanning perhaps half a millennium, had been completed before the Mycenaean civilization was underway. It is clear that a European origin for the European tradition of megalithic building must be sought. Right now, one can look back either to the cist tombs and collective burials of the French Tardenoisian coastal Mesolithic, or to the widespread and possibly early northern European mortuary house-and-barrow burial tradition.

• THE FOUNDATIONS OF INDO-EUROPEAN SOCIETY

The discussion thus far has concentrated on the evolution of successive subsistence strategies in prehistoric temperate Europe and their correlates in terms of environmental adaptations and social arrangements. It is in the second half of the third millennium B.C. that we have the first clear indications of another major step in economic development: the change from shifting to settled agriculture. This is essentially the agriculture of later prehistoric and early historic Europe. While scarce, there is evidence of ploughing from the Late Neolithic, and of manuring, permanent forest clearance, and permanent fields from the Bronze Age onwards. Such considerable investments of labor in the land may be expected to have had sociopolitical consequences. In consideration of the growing importance in the European Bronze and Iron Ages of fortified sites and warrior and ruler burials, and of the sociopolitical structure of protohistoric Europe as gleaned from classical sources and oral traditions, it is tempting to relate the emergence of local chiefdoms and hierarchically organized societies to the developing forms of land tenure, allocation, and defense required by permanent settlement and increased agricultural capability.

However, if one interprets the archaeological evidence by following traditions known from the ethnohistoric horizon backward in time and space, these institutions can be regarded as expressions of an Indo-European ancestry, and of a barbarian Europe's "heroic" outlook. Pattern rather than process is of paramount importance in this view, which considers ethnohistoric, linguistic, and archaeological evidence and emphasizes recurring features. Turning to the ethnohistoric record, for example, it can be argued that medieval feudalism shared with other societies of early historic Europe a hierarchical structure of graded obligations from chieftain down through warrior to free men and commoners. These obligations were in essence personal and not territorial. Archaeologically, there is clear evidence for similar status differentiation in burials of the Hallstatt and La Tène (Figure 2.3*E–F*) Iron Age cultures of central and western Europe from 730–200 B.C. (these archaeological cultures have been securely identified with the historic Celts), and by extension, in completely prehistoric Bronze Age Europe as well. Using words common to the different Indo-European languages (of which the Celtic languages constitute an important group), philologists have reconstructed aspects of an early Indo-European society which should date to the third millennium B.C., and which would possess a god-king elected from a royal family, a warrior assembly, and a caste of free men. The nature of archaeological evidence permits only limited direct social reconstruction; it is not likely that these inferences can be proven archaeologically. On the other hand, there are observable regularities in material-culture patterning which appear to reach out into woodland Europe from the third millennium B.C. southern Russian steppe, an area which on philological grounds should be associated with the beginnings of Indo-European speech. The trait complex includes mortuary house-and-barrow burial, the association of weapons with burials, wagons and carts, fortified hilltop settlements (later hill-forts), and the domesticated horse. The first appearance of these traits in Europe is in the third millennium B.C., more or less at the same time that we have the earliest evidence for plough agriculture. They are frequently first associated with the "Battle Axe/Corded Ware/Single Grave" complex of Late Neolithic cultures of northern Europe, with which plough agriculture has also been connected. Their last appearance together is in the "chieftains' burials" of the Celtic world.

There is a relationship here, just as there must be between the working of permanent fields and the situation and local distribution of tribal strongholds. But it is dangerous to argue simplistically from material-culture assemblages to language groupings and back again, or deterministically from economic to social systems. The errors and limitations of these arguments are now beginning to be recognized, and a shift to other explanatory hypotheses in the near future can be anticipated.

- BIBLIOGRAPHIC ESSAY

For a general introduction to the climate of Late Pleistocene-Early Holocene Europe, the reader may consult Karl W. Butzer's *Environment and Archaeology*, 2nd edition, published by Aldine in 1971, and R. F. Flint's *Glacial and Quaternary Geology*, published by Wiley in 1971. Bjorn Kurten's *Pleistocene Mammals of Europe*, published by Aldine in 1968, provides a valuable review of faunal data.

J. G. D. Clark's work *Prehistoric Europe: The Economic Basis*, published by Stanford University Press in 1952, remains a very useful source of both data and bibliographic references for terminal Paleolithic and Mesolithic Europe. Readers interested in specific sites of these periods may consult two works by J. G. D. Clark: *Excavations at Star Carr*, published by Cambridge University Press in 1954, and the more recent *Star Carr: A Case Study in Bio-archaeology*, an Addison-Wesley Module in Anthropology, No. 10, 1972. The other main site discussed in this chapter, Stellmoor, is described in A. Rust's work *Die Alt- und Mittelsteinzeitlichen Funde von Stellmoor*, published by K. Wachholtz (Neumünster, West Germany) in 1943; also see Rust's *Das Altsteinzeitliche Rentierjägerlager Meiendorf*, published by K. Wachholtz in 1937.

The appearance and spread of agriculture in southeast Europe are conveniently documented by R. Tringham's *Hunters, Fishers, and Farmers of Eastern Europe: 6000–3000 B.C.*, published by Hutchinson (London) in 1971. Her discussions of individual sites and the extensive bibliography make Tringham's book particularly valuable. Jane M. Renfrew's *Palaeoethnobotany*, published by Columbia University Press in 1973, provides a useful background and reference for all discussions of plant domestication, and contains a comprehensive bibliography of botanical reports from a variety of sites. The reader seeking specific site reports of this period of early agriculture may consult D. Srejović's article "Lepenski Vir—a new prehistoric culture in the Danubian region," in the journal *Archeologica Iugoslavica*, Vol. 7, pages 13–18, published in Belgrade in 1966; B. Soudsky's "The Neolithic site of Bylany," in *Antiquity*, Vol. 36 (1962), pages 190–200; and a more recent article by Soudsky and I. Pavlů entitled "The linear pottery culture settlement patterns of central Europe," appearing in the volume *Man, Settlement and Urbanism,* edited by P. Ucko, R. Tringham, and G. Dimbleby, published by Duckworth (London) in 1971. One should also read R. Rodden's "An Early Neolithic village in Greece," in *Scientific American,* April 1965. Jacqueline Murray's *The First European Agriculture,* published by Edinburgh University Press in 1970, provides a faunal and botanical overview of more than one thousand European sites, while a critical perspective on the evidence for early pastoral economies of northwestern Europe is provided by R. Bradley in "Prehistorians and pastoralists in Neolithic and Bronze Age England," in *World Archaeology,* Vol. 4 (1972), No. 2.

The related problems of Near Eastern and European connections and the recalibration of radiocarbon dates are discussed by C. Renfrew in his book *Before Civilization,* published by Knopf in 1973. A useful background to the recalibration controversy is provided by *Radiocarbon Variations and Absolute Chronology,* edited by I. U. Olsson, and published by Wiley in 1970. Readers interested in the problems surrounding the megaliths of Atlantic Europe are directed to G. Daniel's *The Megalith Builders of Western Europe,* published by Hutchinson (London) in 1958; S. Piggott's *Neolithic Cultures of the British Isles,* published by Cambridge University Press in 1954; C. Renfrew's "Colonialism and Megalithismus" in *Antiquity,* Vol. 41 (1967), pages 276–288; and Renfrew's "Monuments, mobilization and social organization," in the volume which he also edited, *The Explanation of Culture Change: Models in Prehistory,* published by the University of Pittsburgh Press in 1973.

Though now dated, V. Gordon Childe's classic work *Dawn of European Civilization,* 6th edition, published by Routledge and Kegan Paul in 1957, still provides an intellectual background to syntheses of later European prehistory. S. Piggott's *Ancient Europe,* published by Edinburgh University Press in 1965, presents both a highly competent synthesis and a full bibliography. Evidence relating to the later cultures of eastern Europe is summarized by M. Gimbutas in *Bronze Age Cultures in Central and Eastern Europe,* published by Mouton (The Hague) in 1965.

A new overview of France in both earlier and later prehistory is provided by S. Piggott, G. Daniel, and C. McBurney, who edited

France Before the Romans, published by Thames and Hudson (London) in 1974.

Ethnohistorical accounts of northern European cultures in contact with the classical world at various times are provided in the *Agricola* and *Germania* of the Roman historian Tacitus, and in the *De Administrando Imperio* of Porphyrogenitus. Finally, Nora Chadwick's *The Celts,* published by Penguin in 1971, is a convenient introduction to the last phases of European prehistory.

3
THE MEDITERRANEAN
ROBERT RODDEN

Ancient Greeks and Romans commonly held that the civilized world began and ended in the land around the Mediterranean. Consciously or unconsciously, archaeologists have accepted this viewpoint in defining "civilization" and the role of the Mediterranean in human history. The civilizations of the ancient Mediterranean, like their counterparts in the ancient Near East, have been seen as innovative centers, producing inventions, trade networks, ideas, and value systems of which Europe and Africa were in due course the conservative receptors; it has been customary to dwell upon this in interpreting European prehistory. In practical terms, the spread of these traits has constituted the basis for the traditional pan-Mediterranean and European chronological framework.

More recently, archaeologists have been asking questions of the archaeological evidence that extend beyond defining the material-culture antecedents of western European civilization. Fundamental to the new approach is a desire to understand how cultural systems work within themselves, and how various internal and external factors combine to determine the course of their development. Among the most important of the external factors to consider is the role of geography and environment.

• GEOGRAPHICAL AND ENVIRONMENTAL BACKGROUND

One of the greatest proponents of pan-European prehistory was

78

V. Gordon Childe, the preeminent twentieth-century prehistorian and one of the few archaeologists to attempt to view the Near East, the Mediterranean, and continental Europe in one great culture-historical sweep. For Childe, and the culture-historical archaeologists of his day, the land was not seen primarily in terms of human settlement, but rather as the determining factor in directing the movements of peoples and ideas; thus mountains were viewed as barriers, and sea-ways, coastal plains, and rivers as corridors in this process. Following Childe, others have described the land in terms of selected environmental resources to be exploited, either by hunters and gatherers, farming communities, or trader-metallurgists. Such studies can be criticized to the degree that their oversimplicity tends to exaggerate the static and one-way nature of environmental adaptations and the "single-mindedness" of primitive economies. Archaeologists today believe in looking for the developing strategy of human responses to a combination of environmental factors: relief, climate, soil, vegetation, and fauna. This is particularly important in such a topographically varied and environmentally diverse area as the Mediterranean.

In contrast to the broad plains and extensive highland areas that characterize much of continental Europe and Africa, the relief of the land bordering the Mediterranean is small in scale. In Greece, Italy, the Iberian Peninsula, and North Africa, the topography tends to be a complex mosaic of closely juxtaposed mountains, valleys, plains, and sea; this diversity is a legacy of mountain building that began in the Mesozoic with the pushing up of the Pyrenees, Alps, Balkan Highlands, and Atlas Mountains and that has continued inside the borders thus defined up to the present time. Many of these mountains are made of rapidly erodable sedimentary rocks; this fact, combined with the Mediterranean climate and vegetation, has led to a profile of jagged peaks, deeply incised river valleys, and comparatively flat-bottomed alluvial plains, very few of which front directly onto the Mediterranean coast. In many places in the northern Mediterranean, mountains extend right to the coast and even out to sea in the form of island chains, as in the Aegean or along the Yugoslav Dalmatian coast. Major islands, each with their own mountains, major valleys, and restricted plains, are Crete, in the eastern Mediterranean, and Sicily, Malta, Corsica, and Sardinia in what has traditionally been called the western Mediterranean.

The intimate relationship between local topographical diversity and differences in climate greatly influences the nature of vegetation cover and the nature of human exploitation of biotic resources in the Mediterranean. This relationship has also made it difficult to define Mediterranean climate by any single criterion. The definition that we have chosen is the one that bears most directly on the formation of soil and the nature of plant growth, whether native or cultivated. Map 3.1 shows the distribution of the different Mediterranean bio-climates using this definition. The overall picture is one of a climate with hot, dry summers and relatively mild winters, with rainfall mostly in the autumn and spring and extremely sparse in summer. This picture is modified according to local altitude and, over larger areas, by prevailing winds: moist air from the Atlantic generally means that the western coasts of Iberia, Italy, and Greece have more rain and therefore denser vegetation than the eastern coasts; cold air from central Europe and Turkey effectively limits the extension of Mediterranean plants in the Balkans; and hot air from the Sahara makes much of the North African coastline practically a semidesert.

A great variety of plant communities is presently found within the zone dominated by the Mediterranean bio-climates. At altitudes up to about 800 meters, evergreen forest or, in less favored areas, primary *maquis,* represents the stable or "climax" development of the Mediterranean climate. The former is generally dominated by evergreen oaks or pines, with a lower layer of small-leaved evergreen shrubs, and a field layer of perennial herbaceous shrubs. *Maquis* or *macchie* (literally, bush) occurs typically in the form of high, dense thickets of evergreen shrub. Above 800 meters in most places lies a deciduous forest zone with deciduous oaks, hornbeam, chestnut, beech, and ash. At the highest altitudes (above 1800 meters) subalpine coniferous forests or meadows occur. Man has had a profoundly disturbing effect on the lower-altitude climax vegetation, and today evergreen forest and primary *maquis* are a feature only of the more inaccessible and protected regions. In their place are widespread areas of debilitated land with secondary scrub and steppe vegetation.

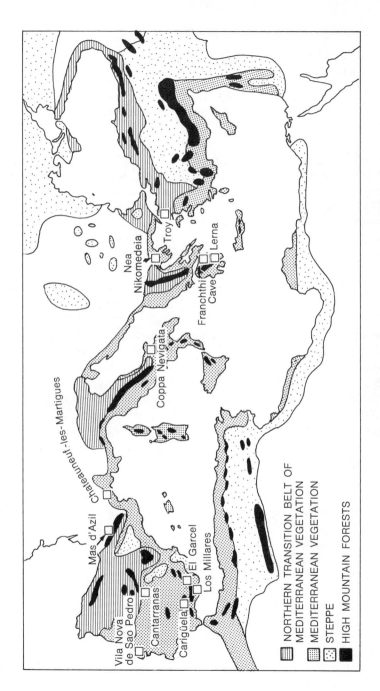

MAP 3.1   Vegetation areas and selected sites of the Mediterranean basin.

NORTHERN TRANSITION BELT OF
MEDITERRANEAN VEGETATION

MEDITERRANEAN VEGETATION

STEPPE

HIGH MOUNTAIN FORESTS

Mas d'Azil

Chateauneuf-les-Martigues

Troy

Nea
Nikomedeia

Franchthi
Cave

Lerna

Coppa Nevigata

Vila Nova
de Sao Pedro

Cantarranas

Cariguela

El Garcel

Los Millares

• ETHNOGRAPHIC ANALOGY: LAND USE AND
CULTURE AREAS IN HISTORIC TIMES

How have these features of the natural environment been used
within historic times, and how have they affected cultural patterning for the period for which written or ethnographic records exist?
Such information is vital for constructing models of social and
economic behavior in the prehistoric past.

Over much of the Mediterranean area, the location of encampments, farmsteads, villages, and larger communities—whether historic or prehistoric—is determined largely by permanent water
supply. The markedly seasonal nature of the rainfall and the poor
water-holding capacity of Mediterranean soils and vegetation leave
all but the major rivers dry in the summer months; the only permanent sources of water are springs or wells in dry stream-
bottoms. Scarcity of water does not determine the location of
occupation sites at higher altitudes and latitudes, where permanent
streams are more a feature of the landscape.

As a general rule, the lowland alluvial and coastal plains around
the Mediterranean are best adapted to the cultivation of winter
crops and summer fruits; arable and mixed farming have long been
the traditional economy in these areas. Where environmental conditions are not favorable to tillage, pastoralism (mixed with cultivation where possible) is the dominant economy. This pastoralism
is based upon sheep and goats, because the Mediterranean herbage
is too coarse for successful cattle rearing. Transhumant pastoralism,
involving the seasonal movement of the animals between mountain
and lowland pastures, is another traditional feature of the Mediterranean economy and is directly related to the close juxtaposition of
upland and lowland regions. The transhumants of Mediterranean
regions follow temperate conditions in their seasonal migration:
in the summer they pasture their flocks in the cooler, moister
mountain highlands, and in the winter they move to lower altitudes
when temperate conditions have replaced the parched, dry summers. Characteristically, these transhumant movements involve
short-distance ascents. In certain areas, as in Spain, at the mouth
of the Rhône, and in the Yugoslav Adriatic hinterland, they involve horizontal long-distance movements having much in common

with the seminomadic movements of Near Eastern and North African pastoralist groups. A significant feature of Mediterranean pastoralist movements is that they commonly transcend traditional social and cultural boundaries.

These boundaries occur frequently throughout much of the Mediterranean. They reflect the multiplicity of what traditionally have been termed "culture areas" as well as the role that the complex relief and environment play in defining the boundaries of social and economic intercourse. One consequence of such small-scale differentiation is the reinforcement of patterns of local or subregional economy of the sort witnessed in the Balkans today, in the small feudal kingdoms and dukedoms of medieval Mediterranean Europe, and in the maritime republics of Italy. A second consequence is the polythetic or nonaligned and continuously variable direction and intensity of cultural relationships.

• POST-PLEISTOCENE CLIMATIC AND ENVIRONMENTAL CHANGE

One of the thorniest problems facing prehistorians and historians today is the cause-and-effect relationship in the past between climatic change, environmental change, and man's exploitation of his natural resources. For the Mediterranean area we have some historical accounts upon which to draw for information for the past 2500 years, but for earlier periods, and for areas not mentioned by classical or medieval writers, the burden of elucidating these interrelationships must be assumed by paleontologists and geomorphologists. It has been argued that parallel climatic episodes affected the Mediterranean region and western Europe in the Late Pleistocene and post-Pleistocene: that the glacial maxima of the Late Pleistocene in northern Europe were marked in the Mediterranean area by pluvial periods and that after 9000 B.C., in postglacial times, there were comparable correspondences between the more minor but well-documented climatic oscillations of northern Europe and climatic changes in the Mediterranean area.

These simple climatic correlations, which were in large part assumed by earlier workers in the absence of any paleobotanical information from the Mediterranean, have been controverted by the first results of systematic studies in many different Mediterranean areas. The picture that is beginning to emerge is complex indeed, and as might be expected, detailed correlations even between different parts of the Mediterranean cannot be made. In contrast to what was previously supposed, accumulating evidence argues for a cold and *dry* climate in many Mediterranean areas; it also suggests that in post-glacial times, while minor fluctuations in temperature and precipitation may have occurred, the most effective agent of vegetational change may have been man. Classical sources document the rapid degeneration of primary vegetation through deforestation, brushwood cutting for fuel and charcoal, and overgrazing in ancient Greece.

• POST-PLEISTOCENE HUNTERS AND FISHERS

It has already been noted that the onset of post-Pleistocene climatic conditions does not appear to have altered environments in the lands bordering the Mediterranean in the ways that it did in continental Europe. One might therefore tend to assume that in the Mediterranean region the life-style of post-Pleistocene hunters and gatherers might not have differed radically from that which preceded it. In many dimensions of culture this appears to be true, more or less. For example, in many areas the local Late Paleolithic tool kit continued with few modifications. But too much emphasis on the continuity of culture neglects some of the more consequential economic innovations in the history of recent man in Europe and ignores adaptations which as new departures are now exciting the research interests of archaeologists. For the first time in prehistoric Europe, the post-Pleistocene hunters and gatherers of the Mediterranean accomplished an expansion of the food base to include a number of new items; by their nature, these items reflect the regular utilization of resources which previously were largely neglected. The new economic activities include the gathering of land-snails in quantity, the collection of marine shellfish, and offshore fishing; in most areas there is a notable increase in the hunting of small game animals. The question of temporal priority in the systematic exploitation of these resources is an important one; unfortunately, at the present time precise dating is difficult.

Franchthi Cave, a newly discovered site in southern Greece with a long succession of Late Paleolithic, Mesolithic, and Neolithic occupation levels, may provide a sequence for the eastern Mediterranean. The Late Paleolithic levels may date earlier than 9000 B.C.; the Mesolithic levels are radiocarbon dated to 7500–7000 B.C., and the Neolithic levels to 5800–5200 B.C. and later. Preliminary studies of the fauna suggest a Late Pleistocene hunting pattern based almost exclusively on large animals: deer, asses (?), cattle or bison, and large goats. The Mesolithic occupants of the cave hunted deer in large quantities, and pigs and bovids as well. But particularly noteworthy here is the fact that in some samples of the upper part of the cave's Mesolithic deposits, the remains of large fish constitute more than half the total of recovered bone; this indicates an increased reliance on fish, and on the sea, as a source of protein. Elsewhere in the Mesolithic the occupation debris is composed almost exclusively of land-snails. At this site, seashells (limpet and topshell) are found even in the Paleolithic deposits; limpet and *Cerithium* were gathered by the Mesolithic people, but in smaller quantities than the land-snails. In terms of the exploitation of the local marine littoral, it is significant that the range of shellfish species eaten is much greater in the Neolithic than in the Mesolithic; and in addition to the shellfish collected in earlier times, cockles, carpet shells, Noah's Ark shells, and oysters were collected.

In mainland Italy and Mediterranean France, where many more Mesolithic sites are known, the picture is also one of broadly based economic diversity. At some sites molluscs, both terrestrial and marine, and small animals played a more important role in the diet, while at others big animals were still the basic source of food. Boar, ibex, and deer were the predominant large animals hunted in northern and central Italy during the Mesolithic, while ass, horse, and cattle were the principal forms hunted in the south. At Arene Candide on the Italian Riviera the Mesolithic adaptation included the extensive hunting of birds. In Italy the sequence of development of new resources approximately parallels that from Franchthi

Cave. Shellfish have been recovered from many southern Italian sites, such as the Grotta del Cavallo; here they were found in the occupation levels of the Late Paleolithic Romanellian culture. However, it is with the post-7000 B.C. Mesolithic occupation of this and other sites that molluscs really appear in large quantities. In the more continental parts of southern France the exploitation of reindeer for food and antler during the Late Paleolithic gives way to the hunting of red deer during the Mesolithic.

What is the meaning of these shifts in exploitative patterns? And what is their impact on other aspects of the Mesolithic way of life? The replacement of reindeer by red deer in parts of southern France, or indeed at a later date the partial or complete substitution of sheep and goat husbandry for big-game hunting, may reflect successive adaptations to changed environmental conditions; but something more seems to be involved in accounting for the wide-spectrum quality of the new economy. Demographic and social factors may be important in this regard. Semipermanent or permanent settlement is closely associated everywhere with the new pattern of land use. At cave sites this is manifest in the thick accumulations of occupation debris in comparatively short periods of time. On open sites it is apparent in the formation of Mesolithic shell middens. Two such examples are Sidari in northern Corfu and Coppa Nevigata, on the southern Italian Adriatic coast.

The relationship between the Mesolithic hunter-fishers and the Late Paleolithic antecedents is seen most clearly in the chipped-stone technology. In most areas there is a demonstrable continuity between Late Paleolithic and Early Mesolithic tool kits. (For examples from such tool kits, see Figure 3.1.)

In peninsular Italy the Mesolithic tool kit is, with modification, a continuation of Upper Paleolithic traditions with a greater emphasis upon microliths. While quite variable from place to place, the Upper Paleolithic of mainland Italy is essentially an industry of backed blades, burins, and thumbnail scrapers. This continues into and throughout the Mesolithic to such an extent that archaeologists have considerable difficulty in certain areas in distinguishing Late Pleistocene from early post-Pleistocene assemblages. That there are some changes, however, is suggested by the increase in denticulated (serrated), notched, and pointed tools in northern

FIGURE 3.1   The Paleolithic and Mesolithic in the Mediterranean
basin.   (A) Upper Paleolithic stone implements.   (B) Mesolithic
stone geometrics.   (C) Hunting scene carved in rock in Sicily.

and central Italy. At the site of Coppa Nevigata we have an example of the modification of a tool kit of clearly Upper Paleolithic ancestry to include beaked awl implements; experiment has demonstrated that these were adapted to the opening of shellfish, which were found in great quantity at the site.

A comparable continuity between Upper Paleolithic and Mesolithic is evident in southern France and Mediterranean Spain. The Azilian, an early post-Pleistocene industry with a primarily inland distribution in southwestern France, but with outliers in the French and northeastern Spanish Mediterranean zone, is the industry most clearly descended from an Upper Paleolithic tradition, in this case the Magdalenian. The Azilian is characterized by a high proportion of thumbnail scrapers, "Azilian points," and flat harpoons, all of which are features in some form of the Magdalenian industry; like the Magdalenian, the Azilian is a blade-based industry. It differs from the former in the conspicuous absence of burins and by the presence of triangular and lunate microlithic elements.

Along the French Mediterranean littoral and the Spanish Mediterranean coastlands, the available evidence suggests continuity from Upper Paleolithic through Mesolithic, much as in peninsular Italy. Again, different regional and subregional expressions of what is essentially an Epigravettian tradition appear to be involved. For example, it is questionable whether the cultural succession Romanellian-Montadien-Castelnovian strictly applies outside the French Midi, although there can be very little doubt that the general course of development of the Mesolithic tool kit followed roughly comparable lines in adjacent areas.

The appearance of microlithic trapezoidal arrowheads is one innovation of the later Mesolithic of the western Mediterranean that crosses regional boundaries, and yet appears to be alien to the native Italian and western Mediterranean Mesolithic traditions described above. It is traditionally associated with the temperate European Tardenoisian Mesolithic. The radiocarbon age determinations dating the first occurrences of trapezes in the wider southern European area align them and their associations with the Late Mesolithic and Early Neolithic of Greece and the Balkans, where the type is earlier present.

Greece seems to present a notable exception to the general rule that Mediterranean Mesolithic tool-making traditions are rooted in local Upper Paleolithic ones. As in peninsular Italy, the Upper Paleolithic/Late Pleistocene industries of Greece are characterized by a tool kit that is based on the backed blade and bladelet; geometric microlithic forms (crescents and triangles) are common, as is the use of the micro-burin technique and the presence of large asymmetrical curved or shouldered points. By about 7000 B.C. at Franchthi Cave in southern Greece, however, the tool kit is very different in character. Backed forms are virtually lacking from the industry, as are the typical curved points. Instead, notched spokeshave-type flakes are found; these are a major element in the Late Paleolithic-Mesolithic chipped-stone tradition of the northwestern Balkans, as demonstrated at the important stratified cave site of Crvena Stijena near the Dalmatian coast. It is possible that such assemblages constitute the remnants of what is fundamentally a highland, western Balkan Mesolithic chipped-stone tradition. Certainly there is no evidence from the lowland coastal plains facing onto the Aegean for such a tradition. In the latter area, however, next to no Mesolithic sites are known. At the site of Samari on the Plain of Thessaly, the industry is dominated by blades and blade-segments. Such a tool kit is very different from what is known from the Adriatic area of the Balkans, and is very reminiscent of industries from the earliest farming sites in the area.

• THE FOUNDATIONS OF PEASANT FARMING SOCIETY

It has long been assumed by prehistorians that the chief Neolithic arts (domesticated stock and cereals, pottery and polished ground stone tools) were introduced into the Mediterranean zone either by colonization or diffusion from the Near East, and then spread from east to west. Recent archaeological research in all areas of the Mediterranean suggests that such a view does not reflect the pattern and sequence of actual events; rather, it reflects the period in the history of archaeology that was dominated by V. Gordon Childe's migrationist and diffusionist models. Childe and his contemporaries did not have the benefit of radiocarbon dating in their working out of regional sequences and interregional chronologies;

thus they relied primarily on select culture trait comparisons and parallels which they felt to be significant.

Since the 1950s radiocarbon age determinations have increasingly provided the basis for interpreting the patterns of culture change in prehistoric archaeology. The age determinations that have been made for archaeological occurrences in the Mediterranean zone suggest that by about 6000 B.C. we have the establishment of the Neolithic arts in those lands bordering the Aegean and in those environments which are most closely akin to those of Anatolia—Mediterranean Europe's land-bridge to the Near East. By about 4500 B.C. the arts were known throughout the Mediterranean. In using radiocarbon age determinations for the time period between 6000 and 4500 B.C. it is important to realize that the technique provides dates that are independent of the associated cultural material. Because these radiocarbon dates precede the period for which proper tree-ring correlations can be made between radiocarbon ages and true historical ages, the chronology for the foundation and spread of farming in the Mediterranean is, practically speaking, a refined relative chronology; it is not indicative of absolute chronological relationships except in the coarsest sense.

A study of the seventh, sixth, and fifth millennia B.C. radiocarbon-dated occurrences suggests a number of important facts concerning the foundation of peasant village farming society in the Mediterranean bio-climatic zone. First, the general pattern of the spread of farming culture appears to proceed from east to west. Second, significant factors in this spread are local inventions, possibly independent, and environmental adaptations which in themselves are of lasting importance. Third, in many areas the Mesolithic way of life continues after the local beginnings of farming and may become an important element in the total system of land exploitation. Fourth, the processes of cultural change that are involved are complex.

It has recently been argued that the earliest and foundational essays into animal domestication in the nuclear area of the Near East constituted attempts at "banking" reserves—in the form of village flocks—upon which communities could depend in emergency situations. Evidence for the earliest farming economies in the Mediterranean area suggests that animal husbandry, together with cereal cultivation, played an everyday role in what is fundamentally a simple agrarian economy. In this respect the economy of the very first Mediterranean farming groups may be likened to the established agricultural economies of seventh to fifth millennia communities in the Near East, with which they are culturally closely allied, too.

The marked cultural provincialism of the Near East during this period is also characteristic of the Mediterranean. In a very general way three major culture areas can be defined for Mediterranean early farming cultures, each with numerous and not insignificant subdivisions. These could be termed the Aegean, the circum-Adriatic, and the western Mediterranean provinces.

The earliest verifiable village-farming communities in the Mediterranean zone are found in the Aegean and date to between 6000 and 5500 B.C. Already there appear to be regional and subregional differences in cultural tradition and land use. Differences in land use are reflected in site location, type of site, and the character of the faunal and floral remains from the site. For example, village settlement mounds are a feature of well-watered lowland and coastal plains where extensive tracts of good arable land are available. The crops cultivated include wheat, barley, and lentils, and among the domesticated animals (sheep and goat, pigs and cattle) cattle appear regularly to play a more important role than they do on hillside sites. Such a pattern of settlement is the dominant one in northern Greece, where a modified Mediterranean climate may be said to prevail; but it is also found in favorable locales in central and southern Greece and on Crete. In northern Greece settlement mounds the size of small villages are also found on rocky hillsides adjacent to the plains, where the nature of the land is more suitable for grazing and hunting; it can be argued that together the upland and lowland sites represent an exploitation pattern involving short-distance seasonal transhumance. In central and southern Greece—within the realm of the Mediterranean bio-climatic zone *sensu strictu*—the sites which are found on poor soils or rocky slopes are either open settlements or caves.

Our knowledge of domestic architecture and of the actual plan of settlements is limited; what evidence we do have is from settlement mounds and argues for a village made up of closely spaced but detached rectangular dwellings. In concept, such an arrangement is typically European; it is characteristic of contemporary peasant villages in eastern Europe. It is also fundamentally different from the nucleated settlement plan of the seventh millennium B.C. and later in the Near East, where structures are joined to one another around an open courtyard.

The chipped-stone tool kit (Figure 3.2*A*) is another manifestation of the distinction between the Aegean and the Near East. It is based upon blades of flint and obsidian and includes trapezes and snapped segments of blades which were mounted obliquely in sickles or reaping-knives so as to form a jagged cutting edge. This mounting is typical of the Aegean and temperate European Neolithic and should be contrasted with the Near Eastern Neolithic arrangement of flint blade segments end-to-end to form a straight sickle-edge. The obsidian comes from Melos, an island in the central Aegean Cycladic group. This source was utilized not only by the mainland Greek Early Neolithic farmers but also by contemporary communities in Crete and westernmost Anatolia. It is doubtful if an established trading network in obsidian, based on the island, existed at this time.

The art of making pottery among the Aegean farming communities undoubtedly had its first inspirations in the earlier traditions of the Near East. But even at the beginning, important regional differences can be delineated within the area, each with long histories that can be traced locally down to around 4500 B.C. on the Greek mainland, and later on Crete. Neolithic Crete had an ultraconservative pottery tradition based upon dark burnished bowls with incised decoration, the origin of which is one of the great unanswered problems of Aegean prehistory. Certainly it is fundamentally different from the pottery tradition of central and southern Greece; in that tradition, there is a different repertoire of Early Neolithic vessel shapes, and decoration was accomplished either through firing the tops and bottoms of bowls different colors, or by painting red linear designs on a white ground, a technique that developed into the highly specialized Middle Neolithic "urfirnis" decoration. In northern Greece the picture is different again. In various sub-regions at different times during the Early and Middle Neolithic a

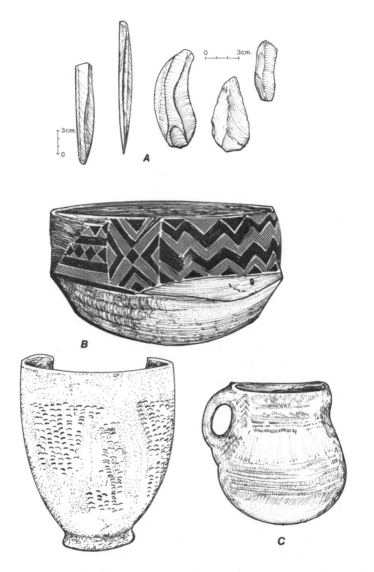

FIGURE 3.2   Neolithic artifacts from the Mediterranean basin.   *(A)*
Stone blades and points.   *(B)* Adriatic pottery.   *(C)* Shell-impressed
pot from Spain.

wider variety of vessel forms were used than elsewhere. Building upon a core tradition of red-on-white painting, numerous individual local styles developed and other forms of pottery decoration, such as impression, and the painting of designs in white on a dark self-colored ground, were borrowed from adjacent areas. About the middle of the fifth millennium B.C. this picture of largely self-sufficient peasant farmers changed to one in which organized trade and interregional contacts became far more important.

Neolithic traits probably first appeared in force in the Adriatic zone of the Mediterranean in the period 5500 to 5000 B.C. Local hunter-gatherer traditions, selected features of Aegean and possibly Northern Balkan Neolithic cultures, independent inventions, and new adaptations are all involved in the configuration of Neolithic culture in this area. Even the earliest Neolithic of the Adriatic zone is not a simple translation into a new region of Aegean or Near Eastern culture, economy, or peoples. The complexity of the quest for Adriatic Early Neolithic origins is seen most clearly in the pottery (Figure 3.2*B*), which from its beginnings possesses the same repertoire of bowl and jar forms as that found in the central and southern Greek Early Neolithic. But this pottery is very distinctly Adriatic in terms of its decoration. From the earliest phases this decoration is carried out primarily by impression on the outside surface of vessels before firing, employing any of a variety of objects for this purpose; most typically, the denticulate edge of the cockleshell is used. Red-on-light painted pottery also occurs, but it is only vaguely reminiscent of the Greek Early Neolithic styles and is found mainly in southern Italy. Subsequently, a variety of new techniques and local styles evolved after 4000 B.C. incorporating both native traits and trans-Adriatic influences. It is possible that the earliest element of Neolithic culture to appear in the Adriatic is pottery, or pottery and stock rearing. By 5500 B.C. pottery is found on the Greek and Yugoslav side of the Adriatic in coastal midden and cave sites, where shellfishing and hunting remained important activities. At about the same time the temperate oak-mixed forest gave way to Mediterranean juniper shrub and mesic trees. In understanding the history of man-land relationships it is of vital importance for paleobotanists to determine through additional work whether this vegetational change represents a change to a warmer climate or whether it represents deforestation by man; in the latter case overgrazing by sheep and goat is probably a contributive factor. Open village settlements appear along this coast only after 5000 B.C. It has recently been argued that on the other side of the Adriatic, in southern Italy, farming was introduced around 5000 B.C. by groups from outside who established themselves in ditch-enclosed settlements in the lowlands and practiced a fully Neolithic way of life, complete with herding and farming. In marginal areas descendants of the native Mesolithic population continued to practice a gathering economy, but in some cases combined it with sheep and goat pastoralism, which subsequently became more and more important. This two-fold economic exploitation of the land continued down until about 2000 B.C., with the major modification being a decline in the gathering of land-snails and certain shellfish and an increase in exclusively pastoralist activities.

In the western Mediterranean the transition from hunting and gathering to settled agriculture is obscure because of the all but complete absence of settlement excavations and radiocarbon dates. The available radiocarbon dates from Mediterranean France and Spain suggest that in those areas the two-fold pattern of land usage, which we have already seen in southern Italy, was well under way by 4500 B.C. In southeastern Spain and southern France most of the Neolithic sites are caves located in hill country away from the coast, usually above small valleys and with limited access to good arable land. The chipped-stone tool kits of these Neolithic cave dwellers indicate that everywhere they are the cultural descendants of local Mesolithic populations. At the site of Arene Candide near Genoa, Chateauneuf-les-Martigues near Marseilles, and the cave of Carigüela near Granada, so-called Mesolithic occupations underlie those with the diagnostic "Neolithic cave culture shell-impressed pottery" (Figure 3.2C). These Neolithic cave dwellers are thought to have been primarily pastoralists, but the presence of grinding equipment and carbonized grains of emmer and einkorn wheat and barley indicate at least some cereal cultivation. At Chateauneuf-les-Martigues the presence of domesticated sheep and goat in the Castelnovian "Mesolithic" levels, and at the Carigüela cave the milling stones in the pre-pottery levels, strongly suggest that the Neolithic economy may have preceded the spread of pottery along these coasts, and possibly is to be associated with the appearance of the trapezes mentioned earlier.

Equally if not more important in the later cultural and economic configuration of western Mediterranean Europe are the lowland Neolithic adaptations behind the southern French littoral and in southeastern and southwestern Spain. It has already been noted that these are poorly known and poorly dated.

In southern France and northern Italy a new pottery tradition called either Lagozza or Chassey appears by about 3200 B.C., and possibly before, succeeding the shell-impressed ware. In the context of the Chassey culture defended open settlement sites and camps were constructed for the first time. The economy is one of mixed farming. The open settlement facies of the Neolithic in the Iberian peninsula is best known from the sites of El Garcel in the southeast and Cantarranas on the southern Meseta near Madrid. At both sites round huts with floors partly excavated into the ground were discovered. Such round houses are a typical feature of Neolithic and later settlements in the western Mediterranean and stand in strong contrast to the rectangular building traditions of the Neolithic in the Aegean and temperate Europe. There is some evidence to suggest a western Mesolithic ancestry for the type. At Cantarranas the associated pottery is not unlike the Chassey ware. At El Garcel a continuation of the local Mesolithic is seen in the chipped-stone tradition, but the pottery differs from both the impressed wares typical of the cave facies and the pottery found at Cantarranas. Sickles, grinding equipment, and underground storage silos argue strongly for the importance of agriculture in these communities. Carbonized cereal grains have been reported from El Garcel, as have olive stones and grape seeds; their presence calls into question the date of what would, on other criteria, have been considered an early site in the area.

With the establishment of peasant farming and herding in the western Mediterranean the base is laid for subsequent economic developments. Given the extractive character of primitive agriculture and grazing, a major factor in this history must have been soil exhaustion and the destruction of much of the climax vegetation: in other words, the formation of the Mediterranean landscape such as we know it today. Thus it is not surprising that more and more evidence argues that groups turned to new economic pursuits and to new resources to complement food production. One manifestation of the broadened economic base is the rising importance of the obsidian sources of the Lipari Islands, Malta, and Sardinia in the Middle and Late Neolithic and their trade throughout Italy and southern France. In Iberia the rich copper-ore deposits of the southern Spanish and Portuguese coasts were exploited early, leading to an established tradition of early metallurgy, trade networks, and a proto-urban situation by about 3000–2500 B.C. Whether environmental and/or demographic changes forced such developments, or whether the primary factor is less tangible and involved the emergence of an expanded world view, is a moot point.

• TRADE AND URBANIZATION

The third millennium B.C. also marks a new period in the Aegean, where an increase in the intensity of cultural life and a new spirit of internationalism signal the beginning of Aegean civilization. The focus of this development is in the maritime, island, and coastal settlements and not in the rich agricultural lands of northern and central Greece. It has been argued that the primary cause was a sudden rise in trade, which increased communication and led to a growth in wealth, a change in weaponry and defense, and new craft specializations. Many would associate the appearance of the new material-culture traits with either the development of a centralized autocracy or the beginnings of direct influences from the older centers of civilization in the Near East. To do so would be to neglect a history of economic, demographic, and social change in which a strong theme is the development of trade and long-distance contact in the Aegean from about 4500 B.C. At about this time the Cyclades are settled and there is an increase in the number and density of settlements on Crete and in southern Greece. Between these settlements there was a measure of intercourse which was lacking in the earlier period of independent farming settlement. It may be tentatively suggested that the catalyst was in part economic: the need for an organized exchange network to handle the newly established trade in the *Spondylus* shell, native only to the Aegean and Mediterranean, and very much in demand for ornaments by contemporary fifth millennium Bandkeramik farming groups in central Europe. One measure of the increased communication is seen in the pottery; for the first time there are precise interregional parallels between mainland and insular Greece, Crete, Anatolia, the northern Balkans, and the northern Adriatic. Another indication is the defensive fortification of settlements immediately accessible from the sea; this is shown by the northern Greek sites of Dimini, where concentric dry stone fortification walls were built, and Nea Nikomedeia, where the Late Neolithic settlement pattern is one of concentric defensive ditches with dwellings crammed in between.

At the core of the genesis of Bronze Age civilization in the Aegean during the third millennium B.C. are the inception of a metal technology and the further development of organized trade and maritime travel. We shall probably never know—nor is it particularly crucial to our understanding of the urbanization process in the Aegean to know—which came first. It is the *combination* of a commodity worth trading and a network for reaching external markets to make that trade profitable that is important. The correlation between the development of a bronze metallurgy (possibly independent of Egypt and the Near East), and the crystallization of concrete trading exchanges between different parts of the Aegean, is striking: around 2500 B.C., bronze weapons (daggers and spearheads) and tools (flat and shaft-hole axes) appear; Early Bronze Age pottery of mainland Greek type is found in the Cyclades and Anatolia; Cycladic folded-arm figurines of marble are found in southern Greece and Crete; and Anatolian two-handled "Depas" cups are found in southern Greece and the Cyclades. This new "international" dimension to the economy created new needs not directly tied to subsistence, but possibly related to it. Craft specialization and the demand for luxury products are witnessed in the richness and variety of artifacts found at Aegean Bronze Age sites. The need for an internal means of organizing production, economic surplus, and defense is impressively documented in architecture: in the Early Bronze Age by the walled towns of Troy, Chalandriani, and Lerna; in the Middle

Bronze Age by the extensive palace-cum-storage complexes of Minoan Crete; and in the Late Bronze Age by the fortified citadel palaces of Mycenaean Greece. Figure 3.3 gives an idea of the vitality of the Aegean Bronze Age.

The Bronze Age civilizations of the Aegean are civilizations without large cities, and with the villages, fields, and pastures of a rural countryside beyond the walls of the "civilized" centers. As in classical and modern times, the society is predominantly agricultural. But, unlike the Neolithic economy, consumption of agricultural products is no longer confined to the farmer himself. The development of agriculture must be considered in the context of a redistributive economy and the demands of both the agrarian and nonagrarian population. During the Bronze Age the olive, the grape, and the fig were brought under domestication. This new arboriculture was particularly important in the later prehistoric development of southern Greece. Specialization in these new crops provided the farmer with additional security through a further diversification of the agrarian economy; as cash crops, they also brought currency into the countryside and involved agriculture increasingly in the process of urbanization. Thus it is that from the Early Bronze Age onward in southern Greece there is an increase both in the number of settlements and in the density of population, while in northern Greece, where the subsistence economy remained based on cereal agriculture and on herding, such increases, while they occur, are much less marked.

• EPILOGUE: HISTORICAL CHRONOLOGIES AND CULTURE PROCESS

In the Mediterranean outside the Aegean, major innovations in the third millennium B.C. and later times frequently have been interpreted either as the work of east Mediterranean colonists or as the result of cultural diffusion from that area. The beginnings of copper metallurgy and of collective burial in built tombs, and the appearance of fortified settlements in the third millennium B.C., have been so interpreted. In the second millennium the establishment of a Mycenaean sphere of influence in the western Mediterranean has been given particular importance; and for the first

FIGURE 3.3   Bronze and Iron Age objects from the Mediterranean.
(A) Bronze axe in the shape of a leopard.   (B) Cycladic figurine.
(C) Cretan gold cup.   (D) Iron Age swords from Spain.

millennium B.C. colonization from the eastern Mediterranean has been considered as a motivating force behind the settlement of the earliest Rome. In arguing pros and cons of such matters precise chronological correlations are of the utmost importance; because the cultural and geographical distances involved between contributor and receiver are so great, the need for a chronology independent of culture-trait comparisons is a particular necessity. Such a chronology is provided by the radiocarbon dating method. Although in earlier periods radiocarbon chronology could only be used as a rather refined means of relative dating, for the third millennium and later the radiocarbon age determination of historically dated objects from Egypt and the Middle East and of tree-rings of known historical age enables us to calibrate radiocarbon dates with true historical ages (Figure 3.4).

The arguments for the overriding importance of local innovation as the dominant agent of cultural change in Mediterranean prehistory have been emphasized here. Thus one might suppose that this chapter will conclude by considering the role that the new chronology—and the re-investigation of long-distance contacts which it is currently stimulating—are playing in demolishing the simplistic invasionist and diffusionist models of cultural change. But archaeological facts preclude a facile conclusion. East Mediterranean faience beads have been found at Fuente Alamo in southern Spain; pottery of mainland Greek Middle Bronze Age date has been found in Sicily; the Sardinian Ozieri culture owes much to its Minoan Bronze Age parentage; Aegean or east Mediterranean Late Bronze Age copper ingots of oxhide form have been found in Sicily and Sardinia; Mycenaean pottery is found in Sicily and southern Italy; and foreign contacts were one important element in the pre-Villanovan, Villanovan, and Etruscan antecedents of ancient Rome.

Such evidence is important in documenting the expanding maritime nature of Aegean Bronze Age trade. But in the context of the later prehistory of the western Mediterranean itself, such contacts are now assuming less importance than before, primarily because the available radiocarbon age determinations leave little room to doubt the vigorous and innovative character of local western Mediterranean developments. As examples, one may cite the

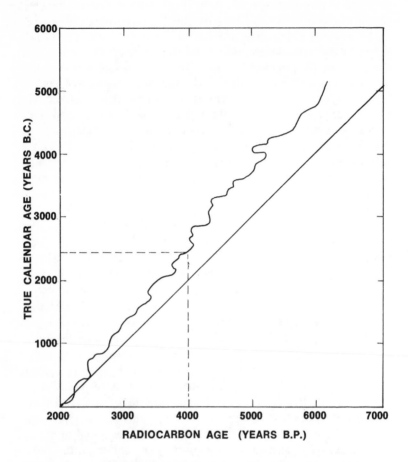

FIGURE 3.4 Suess curve correlating radiocarbon dates with true calendar dates obtained from bristlecone pine tree-rings. To correct a radiocarbon date (routinely given in years "B.P.," Before Present), find its value on the horizontal axis, trace that value upward until the curve is intercepted, then read the equivalent value on the vertical axis in years B.C. The straight line on the graph indicates what the situation would be if radiocarbon years were the same as calendar years.

impressive yet enigmatic tradition of megalithic temple building which arises in Malta well before 3000 B.C. according to the tree-ring calibrated radiocarbon chronology. In Iberia, a copper metallurgy, an extensive trade network incorporating North Africa, and a settlement pattern that includes fortified settlements with semicircular bastions (Los Millares) and chieftains' castles (Vila Nova de Sao Pedro) existed before their Aegean counterparts—if one accepts the dating evidence. Such innovations were important to the people who made them; to define this importance with relation first to native developments, and then to the broader question of culture process and culture change, is the goal of current archaeological explanation in Mediterranean studies.

• BIBLIOGRAPHIC ESSAY

For a general geographical and paleo-environmental background to the Mediterranean basin, the reader is directed again to Karl W. Butzer's *Environment and Archaeology,* 2nd edition, published by Aldine in 1971, and to R. F. Flint's *Glacial and Quaternary Geology,* published by Wiley in 1971. In addition, C. Vita-Finzi's book *The Mediterranean Valleys: Geological Changes in Historic Times,* published by Cambridge University Press in 1972, and the works by E. S. Higgs and Vita-Finzi entitled "The climate, environment and industries of Stone Age Greece," published as Vols. 31–33 of the *Proceedings of the Prehistoric Society* (London) in Part I (1965), Part II (1966), and Part III (1967), provide valuable insights into local ecosystems and the accelerating impact of human cultures on the flora and fauna of the Mediterranean basin.

There is no single introductory text covering the prehistory of the whole Mediterranean area, but a number of books in the "Ancient Peoples and Places" series published by Thames and Hudson (London) provide handy references for particular regions. Some volumes in the series dealing with the northern or European shores of the Mediterranean are L. Pericot-Garcia's *The Balearic Islands* (1972), L. B. Brea's *Sicily* (1966), J. Alexander's *Jugoslavia Before the Roman Conquest* (1965), D. Trump's *Central and Southern Italy Before Rome* (1966), L. Barfield's *Northern Italy Before Rome* (1972), W. Taylor's *The Mycenaeans* (1964), and A. Bernac's *Troy and the Trojans* (1963).

Other works synthesizing later prehistoric data include: F. H. Stubbings' *Prehistoric Greece,* published by Rupert Hart-Davis (London) in 1972; the article by J. L. Caskey entitled "Greece, Crete, and the Aegean Islands in the Early Bronze Age," which appears as Chapter 26-A of the *Cambridge Ancient History,* Vol. I, Part II, published by Cambridge University Press in 1971; J. Courtin's *Le Néolithique de la Provence,* published by the Centre National de la Recherche Scientifique in Paris in 1972; R. W. Hutchinson's *Prehistoric Crete,* published by Penguin (England) in 1962; J. D. Evans' *Prehistoric Antiquities of the Maltese Islands,* published by Athlone (London) in 1971; C. Renfrew's *The Emergence of Civilisation: The Cyclades and the Aegean in the Third Millennium B.C.,* published by Methuen (London) in 1972; and M. Escalen de Fontan's article "Du Paléolithique Supérieur au Mésolithique dans le Midi Méditerranéen," in Vol. 62 (1966) of the *Bulletin de la Société Préhistorique Française.* Most of these works contain up-to-date bibliographies and references to numerous individual sites in their respective areas.

The reader particularly interested in some sites frequently referred to in these sources may consult the following: For Nea Nikomedeia, R. Rodden's "Excavations at the Early Neolithic site of Nea Nikomedeia," in *Proceedings of the Prehistoric Society,* Vol. 28 (1962), pages 267–288; the article "A European link with Chatal Huyuk, uncovering a seventh millennium site in Macedonia, Part I," which appears on pages 564–567 of the *Illustrated London News,* 11 April 1964; and the companion article "Part II, burials and shrines," pages 604–607 of the 18 April 1964 issue of the same journal. For the site of Lerna, see J. L. Caskey's "Activities at Lerna," in *Hesperia,* Vol. 28 (1959), pages 202–207; and for Knossos, see J. D. Evans' "Excavations in the Neolithic mound of Knossos, 1958–60," in the *Bulletin of the Institute of Archaeology of the University of London,* Vol. 66 (1964), pages 4–34.

C. Renfrew's book *Before Civilization,* published by Knopf in 1973, provides a valuable, if partisan, overview of the changes in the interpretation of cultural development in the Mediterranean and northern Europe suggested by the bristlecone pine recalibration of radiocarbon dates.

Thoughtful discussions of some of the problems associated with the study of the prehistory of the Mediterranean area may be found in P. Phillips' article "Population, economy, and society in the Chassey-Cortaillod-Lagozza cultures," in *World Archaeology,* Vol. 4 (1972), No. 1; and in two articles in the same journal, Vol. 2 (1971), No. 3: R. Whitehouse's "The last hunter-gatherers in southern Italy," and M. Jarman's "Culture and economy in the north Italian Neolithic."

The reader interested in some theoretically sophisticated models of culture change in the Mediterranean area may consult the articles by P. M. Dolukhanov, G. Barker, C. Doumas, and M. J. Rowlands in *The Explanation of Culture Change: Models in Prehistory,* edited by C. Renfrew and published by the University of Pittsburgh Press in 1973.

4
THE FAR EAST
JUDITH TREISTMAN

The prehistory of China is as smooth as water-washed jade and as variegated in color. As the archaeologist peels off the layers of deposits, "layers" of cultural styles, possessing an apparent homogeneity, are exposed. The similarities, sometimes in house type, often in art or even in burial practices, are quite remarkable; they cause the prehistorian to invoke models of diffusion-and-migration and of developmental stages, and thus to "explain" the unknown past. Alternatively, when the diversity that underlies the sameness is exposed, the ecological model of cultural adaptation is called forth. China is of course no exception to the futility of using any single approach to prehistory; but perhaps because of the scanty, fragmentary, raw data with which the archaeologist must be content, it is necessary either to devise a rational eclecticism in theory building or to eschew theoretical frameworks altogether and rest with a simple description of available information.

With the founding of the People's Republic of China in 1949, Chinese archaeology was encouraged and given a new direction. The years of illegal and profitable grave robbing and despoiling came to an end; under government sponsorship local field archaeologists were trained in large numbers to survey and rigorously excavate sites that were brought to the attention of specialists in museums and academies. A vast amount of archaeological information became accessible, first to the people of China, and eventually to Western scholars. From simple legislation protecting

106

and preserving archaeological sites and monuments, the government moved into a campaign of education that combined an emphasis on pride in the national heritage with more contemporary themes emphasizing class struggle and the contribution of Chinese peasants and artisans to history.

Two currents seem to be running through Chinese archaeology, especially since the Cultural Revolution began in 1966. One represents an attempt to reinterpret all data in the well-known framework of the historico-political stages—Primitive Society-Slave Society-Feudal Society—while the other seeks an internal analysis of each site. The latter approach is producing excellent field reports, including stratigraphic and palynological details, and illustrative material of very high quality. A few radiocarbon dates have been published since 1972, and it appears that the technique was in use earlier. However, the dates are as yet insufficient to produce a fine chronological grid for ordering sites within periods, and therefore critical shifts in cultural behavior are missed. The absence of a refined chronology is underscored by the tendency of the Chinese scholars to group together large numbers of sites on the basis of a few typological traits and to assign one date and "culture" name to all of them.

The new approach of Chinese archaeologists also seems to emphasize heavily technological history and the analysis of processes and techniques of manufacture. The studies of this sort, especially of ceramics and metals, have been very significant. The same approach has been applied to architectural history with very useful results. But these advances indicate a shift of attention away from prehistory toward historical archaeology, and one consequence seems to be that the theoretical framework within which prehistorians work is poorly developed.

One scheme for handling the uneven data has been to transpose the concept of a "nuclear area" from the Near East to northern China and to trace cultural horizons as they spread over most of the country. This chapter substitutes instead a multifocused image in an attempt to convey the complexities that prepare us for the further complexities of historical China. There are similarities that appear to unite vast spaces during certain periods of prehistory, but these are the fundamental similarities of sociotechnology—the cultural reinterpretation of environment. They should not disguise the creative micro-adaptations that have always occurred.

In order to escape the territorial strictures implicit in the modern political unit of China it is convenient to separate out six regions that have demonstrated cultural adhesion through time. This essentially "nonnuclear" approach in turn permits us to see Chinese prehistory in relation to other regions, not normally considered to be "China."

• TUNGPEI

The geographical essence of the Tungpei is the great Manchurian Plain, surrounded by mountains but opened in the south towards Liaoning and cut by three major rivers: the Nonni, the Sungari, and the Liao. Although the plain today is a region of shifting sand dunes and salt marshes, the fauna associated with the immediate post-Pleistocene period are of the steppes and woodlands. Where grass now covers the plains, forests once stood, punctuated by freshwater ponds and lakes. The populations that inhabited the area during the thousands of years between the end of the Pleistocene and approximately 2000 B.C. possessed a uniformity of lifestyle that was created as a primary technological response to open woodland ecology. It is possible to see at least four micro-adaptations within this uniformity.

1. The Ang-Ang-Hsi aspect (including the site of Shabarak Usu), most typical of the Manchurian plain, is represented at sites located on the remnants of ancient river terraces or on the shores of lakes. The woodlands and water were exploited with a basic forest technology, shown in the tool-making tradition of preforming conical and prismatic cores from which tiny, knife-like flakes were removed. This tradition, which spread throughout the Tungpei (reaching into Shansi province) and the Gobi, was widely distributed in the north; it was also found in the region of Lake Baikal and along the upper reaches of the Amur River. Fishing, gathering of freshwater molluscs, and some hunting of small game sustained the people, although there is still no indication that their dwelling sites were permanent. In the late phases of the Ang-Ang-

Hsi aspect, an intensified utilization of vegetal foods can be recognized through the presence of grinding stones and querns.

2. The flaked-stone tradition spread eastward to the Linhsia region, where it is again found in a forest-efficiency complex even more strongly reminiscent of the Siberian "Serovo." The pottery that was made at this time was not impressed or stamped, and was usually round-bottomed.

3. On the coast itself, subsistence was at first based on a generalized gathering and hunting economy, but by about 1000 B.C. the economy was specialized in the collection of the littoral fauna, especially shellfish and waterbirds. Along the bays and estuaries large settlements grew up where the fishermen were able to trap migrating tuna and other species.

4. In the southern part of the Tungpei, in Jehol and Liaoning, the forest efficiency of the north was transformed into a basic agricultural efficiency. The details of this transformation are not yet clear, but as a technology of cultivation developed, an abundance of earth-working tools—such as polished shouldered-and-grooved hoes and concave "shovels," semi-lunar slate sickles, and stone querns—appeared along with evenly faceted tiny lamellar blades. Samples of the larger Neolithic tools are shown in Figure 4.1*A*. The domestication of animals, notably the use of cattle to draw stone-tipped ploughs, may have been part of this technology. The demographic and cultural stability achieved by plough cultivation (probably of millet, Figure 4.1*B*) lasted several thousand years. Near southern Manchuria and the Ordos region of the Huangho, the adaptation to an agricultural economy was incomplete; a mixed forest efficiency and cultivation of grasses persisted until the region was incorporated into the economy of pastoral nomadism.

The metallurgical industry that appeared in this region of Asia was either introduced from further south, in China itself, and spread across the western steppes, or it developed indigenously. It depended on the increased cultural and economic interaction of specialized groups and individuals. In turn, this brought about some of the sociopolitical rearrangements that laid the foundation for the rise of the great barbarian alliances of the first millennium B.C. Two patterns of settlement seem to have coexisted. As yet these cannot be explained in terms of environmental determinants;

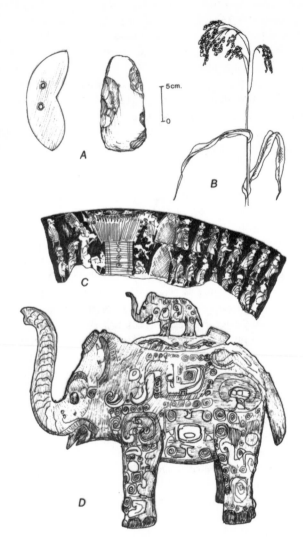

FIGURE 4.1   Early Chinese archaeological phenomena.   *(A)* Heavy
tools from the Neolithic—slate sickle, heavy axe.   *(B)* Millet, an
early Chinese domesticate.   *(C)* Dongson bronze drum fragment.
(D) Ceremonial bronze vessel.

they may have been maintained by cultural necessity. One was characterized by large hilltop villages; these were occupied by farmers who traveled out to their fields, cultivated with animal-drawn bronze or stone ploughshares, and kept domesticated swine in large numbers. Some of the millet fields (possibly wheat was also grown) were irrigated, although not extensively. The second pattern was centered on a complex of domesticated animals; horses and camels were used to provide the mobility needed to maintain control over mixed herds of cattle and sheep. These different patterns of economic activity and the routines of living created a specialization, and perhaps also stratification, of social units which were woven into a larger cultural system. This was achieved by a shared ritual and symbolic communication that we find expressed both in a pervasive art style—the famous animal art—and in an attitude toward the meaning of death that was the basis for a unique stone-slab grave complex.

The sources that stimulated the politicization of the Neolithic relationships were varied; at times the influence of the Mediterranean Near East seemed to dominate, at other times that of continental Europe. Basically, however, politicization stemmed from the inner tension between the two minor traditions; it was against this backdrop that the drama of the formation of Chinese civilization unfolded.

• SOUTHWEST CHINA

There is no clear-cut topographic or cultural demarcation between southwest China and interior mainland southeast Asia. The entire region is characterized by high rugged mountains, strong rivers that course deeply but have fairly broad alluvial plains, heavy subtropical forests, and open parkland. Guided by this topography, the forest-efficiency complex of the region developed two foci, more complementary than mutually exclusive. One focus was on vegetation, and led to casual experimentation with cultivation. The other, in the zone of riverine adaptation, frequently was completely unrelated to agriculture.

There is no radical difference between the stone-tool assemblages of these foci, nor is there a change in the basic manufacturing techniques that seem to persist from the Paleolithic. Viewed chronologically, the developing technical approach to the medium of stone demonstrates a rather flat curve from the chopper-chopping tool industry through the "Hoabinhian," followed by the fully polished axes and adzes of the later Neolithic. These pebble and large flake tools were also used in historically known times, coexisting with iron. It is obvious that the most flexible materials, bamboo and cordage, which are archaeologically absent, must also have been fashioned into a wide range of efficient tools.

During the period of the forest efficiency the riverine focus maintained its generalized character, although by about 5000 B.C. certain specialized adaptations to micro-environments had developed. At first people lived in rock shelters located near the streams that provided an abundance of fish and molluscs. Later, open settlements with midden accumulations show evidence of even more intensive shellfish collecting and a small increase in the hunting or trapping of deer, wild boar, and elephants. Facing away from the rivers, on the hill slopes and in the forests, there was an emphasis on the collection of vegetal foods and the "encouragement" of certain plants and trees. A typical complex of these plants has recently been found in northwestern Thailand (Spirit Cave) in an archaeological context dated at about 11,000 B.C., or earlier. It included pepper, areca nut, candlenut, bottle-gourds, and cucumber, and even peas and beans. In Yunnan province, China, there is evidence of similar experimentation and, at a much later date, some casual cultivation of cereal grasses, notably wheat.

From the time of post-glacial changes in sea levels and the minor alterations in climate that took place from about 12,000 years ago to about 5000 years ago, the cultural image of southeast Asia was a reflection of the quiet and gradual outgrowths of a substantially well-adapted forest efficiency. There were no major population movements, but rather a continual "filling up" of space by self-replicating social groups. Once again, the technological mechanism that triggered more abrupt change in social and political arrangements was the development of a native metallurgical industry. The indigenous bronze-casting craft of central southeast Asia has been documented in its early phases at about 3000 B.C. Although bronze was insignificant in fundamentally altering ecological relationships (only with iron tools did agricultural technology become dominant), it did foster a transregional network for the procurement of raw materials and the production and redistribution of metal goods. As a result, communications in greater southeast Asia broadened in scope beyond the fragmented village, and a shared life-style evolved.

In China itself, localized expressions of this tradition (sometimes called by the name originating in Indo-China—"Dongson") flourished in Szechwan and Yunnan (Figure 4.1C). On the Chengtu plain in Szechwan, for example, a loose confederacy of social groups became internally stratified and politicized as one unit, the Shu, and came to control the exploitation of certain natural resources, such as tin and salt. About 1000 B.C., when the very fertile plain was more intensively cultivated, interaction between the agriculturalists and the pastoralists of the western mountain and grassland zone increased. The Shu apparently came to mediate between these different cultures, facilitating the passage of metal technology from the southwest, consuming and redistributing the surplus production of the sedentary agriculturalists, and at the same time accumulating "wealth" in the form of manufactured commodities, especially ceremonial bronze vessels (Figure 4.1D). Although many of these were prestigious imports from the north (western Chou) and the steppelands, others were distinctively in the southeast Asian tradition.

Similarly, in Yunnan the mosaic ethnic pattern emerged out of the forest efficiency that had permitted successful local specialization to a wide spectrum of micro-environments. The fragmented village way of life persisted: populations apparently did not aggregate but ramified. However, a political-economic stratification did occur on the local level. In a Tien cemetery, for example, this stratification is represented not only by the differentiated burials of chiefs, "warriors," and farmers, but in the kinds of grave goods buried with the chief: gold jewelry and utensils that only he could display; the regalia of horsemanship that perhaps signified his military and political command; and the profits of mercantilism, including bronze vessels (Figure 4.2A) that held strings of cowrie and exotic imports from Indo-China, central Asia, and northern China. Such stratification seems to have coincided with the multi-

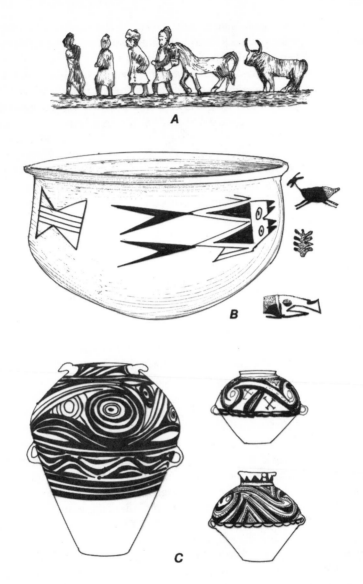

FIGURE 4.2   Chinese pottery and grave goods.   *(A)* Ritual scene from bronze vessel.   *(B)* Pan P'o pot and selected motifs.   *(C)* Pan-shan pots.

cropping of the land. Wheat and millet were cultivated, but rice became increasingly important as metal (iron) tools made terracing and small-scale irrigation possible on the hill slopes.

From the archaeology of southwestern China we derive a picture of growing excitement, of a world in touch with the vitality of all southeast Asia and the west, but in a strange sense veiled from the view of the emerging civilizations of northern China.

• HUANGHO BASIN

The agricultural innovation in China took different forms and oc-curred in several places. We have noted the cultivation of nut trees and vegetables in southeast Asia and the attention given to many plants, among them the cereal grasses, in the forests and steppes of the north. To the east, in Japan, it is becoming apparent that the subsistence focus that concentrated on shellfish collecting also made intensive use of a wide range of nuts, perhaps tending se-lected species of trees, and probably cultivating some plants for their starchy roots. Thus far the archaeological record is unclear as to the earliest experiments with seed cultivation in the Far East, and inference must take the place of observed data.

The fertile loess terraces of the middle Huangho and Wei river tributaries afforded early agriculturalists a relatively safe laboratory. They were assured of good drainage, although they suffered from unpredictable rainfall; the open mixed-deciduous forests and tall grass could be effectively cleared with stone axes and fire, and the loess itself could be cultivated with a dibble stick. Although the zone where the wild millets occurred is not yet known, these grasses were well suited for the loessland. Both domesticated varieties, foxtail millet (*Setaria italica* var. *germanica*) and kaoliang *(Andro-pogon sorghum)* are drought resistant and early maturing. They are the staple cultigens even today; the grain is high in nutritive value and the stems are useful for fuel and thatch. Other plants were brought out of the forest-steppe environment to be cultivated in the loessland, especially varieties of the chenopods and plants yielding oil. The success of the early farmers was actually sup-ported by their continued orientation toward the forest and river. Fishing played a very significant role in their subsistence technology, hunting of deer and rodents was even more important than before, and gathering activities (especially of hazelnuts, chestnuts, and pine seeds) added substantially to the diet. Thus began a pattern of exploitation of diverse environments which enabled the success of the agricultural way of life to continue uninterrupted into the present.

Sufficient stability in this new ecological relationship was achieved, and villages in the Huangho and Wei valleys multiplied until all the space technologically accessible to the increasing population was filled. The village way of life was firmly established when populations of about 500 individuals (or up to 200 households) were able to incorporate sufficient land into the agricultural technology so as to remain sedentary over many generations. There is no indication of short-term occupation of village settlements, so it is possible to infer that the land under cultivation was shifted from time to time while the people remained in one place. Houses in the early villages were large and made of mud, straw, and hewn logs; they followed the northern tradition of having southward-facing, low-ceilinged entranceways protecting them from the cold winds, and they were heated by centrally placed fire-pits. For a reconstruction of an early village house, see Figure 4.3*A*. As agriculture gradually became the focus of subsistence activities, local populations grew, probably because children were necessary to the productive technology, and small houses became more prevalent. It can be hypothesized that the bounded territoriality of agriculture was developing into a land-tenure system that gave a new definition to the social unit of the family and a new significance to children in terms of the continuity of descent and ownership. The proliferation of population caused a constant budding-off of tiny hamlets, each a replication of its parent, but involving no increase in technological efficiency.

Innovations in the pottery repertoire were made by the villagers. The idiom of painted motifs—fish, anthropomorphic figures, and geometrics—on fine red ware was added to the gray pots with textured surfaces that characterized the Asian ceramic tradition for millennia. Curvilinear representations, perhaps symbolic of the growing awareness and manipulation of the surrounding vegetation, increased as the village way of life took root in the river valleys. Figure 4.2*B* illustrates a pot and selected motifs from this period.

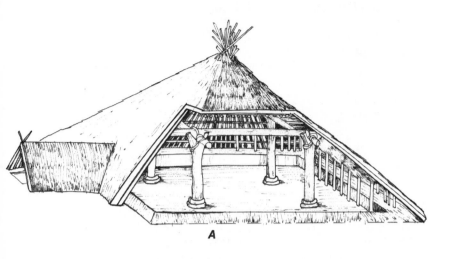

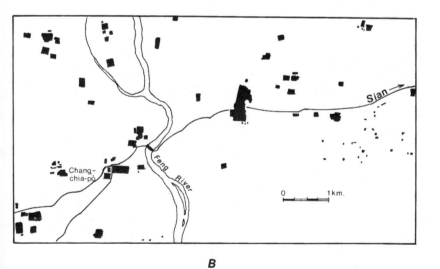

FIGURE 4.3   Ancient Chinese architecture.   (A) Reconstruction of early village house.   (B) Distribution of sites with diversified industrial functions near Sian, Shensi.

• WESTERN SHENSI AND KANSU

The broad region of the Huangho basin must be considered in two parts: the western loessial terraces and the central plains. In the west, especially along the many tributaries of the Huangho system, the pattern of agricultural innovation was altered by the incorporation of another economy, focused on the domestication of cattle, sheep, and goats. In this semi-arid region, the villages that were strung out in the little valleys had at first been self-contained; they could neither optimize cultivation through territorial expansion nor support burgeoning populations. Thus a pattern of semi-nomadism began, involving more people in economic activities centered on grazing mixed herds of animals. A spirit of mobility courses through the region at about 1500 B.C., reaching from the steppes of central Asia into the hills of Shensi. The plain pottery ware of the Ch'i Chia period bursts into a multitude of styles, and the unity of the death ritual expressed in the earlier great hilltop cemeteries of Panshan is broken into a dozen traditions that may reflect growing localized ethnic consciousness. For samples from the pottery of this time, see Figure 4.2C.

The small towns that grew up, such as Ke-hsing-chuang, look ordinary in their archaeological aspect; but a few copper nuggets, a bronze ornament or two, the pits, and the very house floors compacted with the refuse of an intensely variegated economy all hint at a life that must have been interesting and vigorous. The steppe peoples of Asia, constantly moving through the grassland corridors to the west and the highlands of Tibet and southwest China, transmitted impulses that emanated from the worlds of southeast Asia, southern Siberia, and central Asia. Before 1000 B.C. the people of Shensi and Kansu were receiving the products of enclaves of metal workers who were supported by the horse-riding nomads. They themselves soon came to be involved in a complex socio-economic transformation that culminated in the flowering of Chou civilization.

One of the earliest clusters of sites to indicate this transformation is near Sian, Shensi province. Here, at Chang-chia-p'o, were several villages that had become diversified industrial centers. The distribution of these centers is indicated in Figure 4.3B.

There are bone workshops where arrowheads and hairpins were carved, foundries at which the bronze fittings for chariots were manufactured, and sites that specialized in making knives with concave blades and square-looped handles. There are pottery work-shops and kilns that produced roofing tiles for houses. A most important advance in agricultural technology was made when great ceramic rings were used to line the shafts of wells dug into the soft soils. We have no evidence of the mechanisms by which water was raised and distributed, but this is the first clear indication of an attempt to manipulate resources outside of the unpredictable and often insufficient rainfall.

The capital cities of Feng and Hao were occupied for approxi-mately 350 years, a time when Chou interaction with the steppe nomads intensified and forced a politicization of territories. This is apparent in the proliferation of armaments (daggers, swords, and eventually iron-bladed weapons), chariots, and the adminis-trative apparatus necessary to mobilize thousands of men for mili-tary display and threat. The ruling group buried its dead with great riches: horses were dressed in bronze masks and bells, carved-shell plaques, and strings of cowrie; carved and incised jades were placed with the corpse, as well as necklaces of bone, pottery, glass, and bronze beads. These funerals, so reminiscent of the grand tours given the dead rulers of the pastoralists, were sumptuous displays of the commodities of economic wealth, achieved during the lifetime of the individual and memorialized in ritual.

Wu Wang, head of the Chi, led the first expedition against the people to the east (the Shang) in 1122 B.C. and captured their headman, but it took many hundreds of years before the Chou were able to weld the northern cultures into a semblance of a political alliance.

• THE CENTRAL PLAIN

The central plain presents another instance of primary agricul-tural efficiency, one that was perhaps encouraged by a less rigor-ously diversified topography. There, the breakdown of Neolithic self-containment was not the result of interactions with populations that had different technological approaches to subsistence; it developed from an intensification of cultivation. The corresponding growth in populations and the proximity of fissioning villages produced a closed network for the circulation of goods and people. Towns sprang up on the plain; many of them were probably local marketing centers. One of the earliest of these, the town of Ehr Li-t'ou, had clusters of small dwellings, workshops in which simple bronze objects were manufactured, kilns, storage areas, and dug wells. The pottery was a commercial product, wheel made and decorated with complex stamped motifs. A structure of about 100 square meters stood in the town; it had a floor laid over a foundation of layers of tamped earth, and walls of wattle and daub. Many of the burials associated with the town were richly furnished, suggesting that the large building may have been the home of a wealthy family. That a political hierarchy may have been emerging at this time is evidenced by several burials of people who had been bound and mutilated before death.

By 1500 B.C. similar centers of dense populations with satellite villages had appeared all across the plain, extending into the Shantung hills. These retained local identity, although a hint that they were at least marginal to a larger ecumenical style appears in the widespread luxurious black pottery. It is difficult to determine the nature of the circulation of this unique ware; since many of the vessels foreshadow the shapes of ritual bronzes, perhaps they were the hallmark of a religious complex in which a growing class of wealthy families participated. The notion of ecumenism throws the brilliant Shang period into relief and helps to explain the cultural continuity that persisted in the face of that period's explosive eruption.

While it is futile and mostly irrelevant to argue the question of origins, the quality that makes the appearance of the Shang so startling is the aura of elitism for which all preceding events have left us unprepared. The elements that are so intrusive and alien were intimately associated with the ideology and religion of the Shang, and were in fact used to define and reinforce their position at the top of a social hierarchy.

The first city that can be identified as Shang is in northern

Honan province, near Chengchou. This walled city stood at an important crossing of the Huangho. It encompassed almost two square kilometers in area, more than the twentieth-century commercial center. The complex character of Chengchou is best demonstrated by the layout of the cluster of settlements surrounding the walled nucleus of the city. In these settlements were the factories of the potters, the metalworkers, the weavers, the carvers of bone, stone, and wood. The kiln area was near the source of clay and water, on the river banks west of the city wall. The concentration of fourteen kilns, large pits filled with pots waiting to be fired, the use of the fast-turning wheel, and bamboo molds, and the technique of decorating by stamping motifs on the wet clay with carved wooden or ceramic medallions, are all indications that the industry had become specialized, organized for mass production and distribution.

Some of these innovations, made to meet the demands of ceramic specialization, were transferred to the bronze workshops. These especially included advances in kiln construction, control of the firing atmosphere to produce the prevalent uniform grayware, and techniques of molding and decoration. Outside the wall of the city there were settlements that included the foundries and dwellings of the bronze workers. Into simple two-part molds fashioned of clay, molten metal was poured to make arrowheads (Figure 4.4*A*) and socketed axes. The copper in the alloy was almost all locally derived from secondary ores (easily found on or near the ground surface) but tin may have been imported. Many of the earliest vessels were made in multipiece molds; these molds were made from clay models. The decoration found on bronze pieces from Chengchou is all in relief, suggesting that a negative impression had been made in the clay mold in much the same way that pottery was decorated.

The bone workshop was located north of the ancient Chengchou wall; fragments of arrowheads, hairpins, knife handles, fishhooks, awls, and needles were sawed and filed with stone tools, and sometimes carved with small knives of bronze and jade. The materials included buffalo horn, deer antler, and the bones of pigs, oxen, goats, and humans. Figure 4.4*B* shows the style of the carved bone.

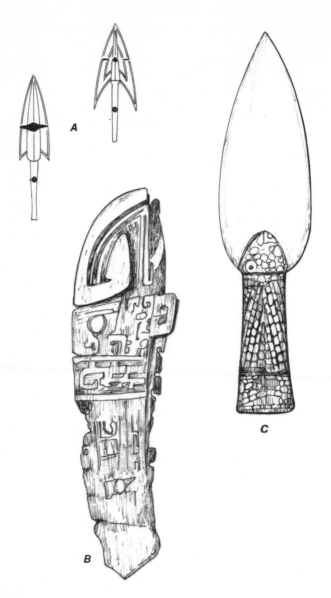

FIGURE 4.4   Remains from the Shang period.   (A) Molded bronze
arrowheads.   (B) Carved bone.   (C) Jade spear head.

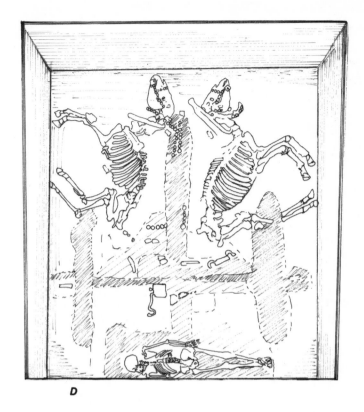

D

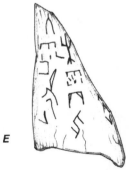

E

FIGURE 4.4 (Continued)   (D) Ceremonial chariot burial.   (E) Oracle bone.

Nephrite (called jade) was ground and polished and then deeply incised with bronze knives. In contrast to bone objects which frequently were entirely covered with incised representations of animals and birds and, later, the same abstract motifs that fill much of the space in bronze decor, jade was treated as a three-dimensional medium. (See Figure 4.4C.)

Although the workshops have not been found, there is archaeological and textual evidence for leather working (especially for armor) and weaving. Bronzes encrusted with the imprint of woven silk fabric have been found in later Shang tombs. Again, the complexity of manufacture suggests that silk weaving was a specialized industrial craft rather than a household product.

The Chengchou city looks like a rather natural development from the central plains intensified farming village complex, but the impetus that led to city development is unclear. It is possible that a political-economic hierarchy emerged as the hundreds of coexisting ethnic groups—many of them now nameless or identified in the histories only as "barbarians"—were brought into the growing administered trade, which was required to sustain incipient industrial specialization. This process of politicization was fully recognized by the Chou rulers, who created a system of tribute and commerce that established territorial boundaries and required managerial control.

The later Shang period, as defined archaeologically by the great complex of palaces, tombs, workshops, and villages at Anyang, does not flow in an easy historical stream from the Chengchou period. Superimposed on the now familiar pattern of clusters of factories and the homes of artisans, and the scattered agricultural hamlets, are the great dwellings and cemeteries of the royal Shang lineage. The ideological emphasis on the sacrificial slaughter of humans and animals is pervasive in the homes of both the living and the dead. The palatial houses are sometimes as large as 60 meters in length, and are almost all built on tamped earth foundations with pillar bases of stone or bronze. Some of the large structures are partitioned, with smaller rooms arranged around central halls. During construction, the three sacrificial animals of the Shang—dog, sheep, and ox—were interred in the foundations. Human guardians with daggers and shields of bronze were sacrificed and buried inside and outside the doors. The cult of sacrifice, presumably a validation of the royal status of the lineage, grew to momentous proportions: in the main compound of Hsiao T'un, there are 852 human victims, 18 sheep, 35 dogs, 10 oxen, and 15 horses.

In the cemetery of royal tombs at Hou Chia Kuang, the great underground chambers (some as deep as 13 meters) are filled with armaments, horses, and skeletons of human beings decapitated during the ritual of sacrifice. Figure 4.4D depicts a chariot burial found at this location. The trappings are not from the agricultural way of life, but clearly derive from northern cultures of which the Shang were a part. The tight organization that carried them to titular leadership of a diverse ethnic world was strengthened by the way in which they realized and formalized their own identity through ritual. The art motifs worked into the ceremonial bronzes were paralleled by a written system of notation, largely devoted to oracular and magical purposes, and an intricate calendrical system which governed the ceremonial cycle. Figure 4.4E shows an oracle bone that was used in Shang ritual.

The thin veneer of Shang civilization spread over northern China but did not succeed in a revolutionary interruption of the sociocultural pattern of the Neolithic. It remained for the Chou to accomplish this transformation through basically political means.

• SOUTH CHINA

In many aspects, the pattern of life that was to characterize most of Chinese history emerged in south China, along the middle and lower Yangtze river valley. This is the pattern created through the complex system of irrigation and terracing, the use of ploughs drawn by water buffalo, and the cultivation of rice.

In the middle Yangtze plain this specialized pattern (possibly deriving from southeast Asia via Szechwan and Yunnan) took hold gradually as it supplanted a previous, sedentary village way of life based on millet agriculture. About 1000 B.C. the cultural phase known locally as Ch'u Chia Ling spread out of the Hanshui Valley to the coastal province of Chekiang and south into Kiangsi,

Fukien, and Taiwan. In the Hangchow bay region, many sites demonstrate an increase in the intensity of agriculture; new crops, such as sesame, beans, peaches, melons, water chestnuts, and even peanuts, appear along with rice. Animal-drawn ploughs tipped with stone shares, stone hoes, and spades, all suggest a complete involvement with agriculture; and the location of villages along streams and lakes, on hillocks and mounds rising 2–10 meters above the plains, indicates that an attempt was being made to manipulate and control the flooding rivers. However, it was not until after the fifth century B.C., when iron agricultural tools were manufactured in this region, that a truly labor-intensive technology developed.

The pottery of the time, the "geometric stamped ware," was widely circulated throughout the southeast, even penetrating into the island world; this circulation reflected the growing crystallization of a shared life style. Many ethnic groups shared in this style while retaining unique cultural identity, and more than one flourishing center of civilization emerged in the south to survive intact for centuries. Ideas and people continued to flow from the south into the greater Pacific region, while the north benefited from its commercial contacts.

This plane of multi-focused organization was the template for much of Chinese history, which in the long run has been moved not by dynasties but by peasants in villages.

• BIBLIOGRAPHIC ESSAY

Barriers of space and language separate most readers from the basic site data of recent Chinese excavations, but happily there are a number of synthetic works by specialists surveying the rich field of Chinese archaeology.

Geographical and paleo-environmental studies of China in western languages are not much in evidence, but the reader may consult the work *Pleistocene and Post-Pleistocene Climatic Variations in the Pacific Area,* edited by D. Blumenstock and published by the University of Hawaii Press in 1966; *The Archaeology and Geomorphology of Northern Asia,* edited by H. N. Michael and published by the Arctic

Institute of North America in 1964; and A. Herrman's excellent *An Historical Atlas of China*, published by Aldine in 1966.

The most detailed accounts of Chinese prehistory and protohistory are to be found in T. K. Chêng's three volumes published by Heffer and Sons (Cambridge, England), namely: *Prehistoric China* (1959), *Shang China* (1960), and *Chou China* (1963). In 1966 the first of these was supplemented by Chêng's *New Light on Prehistoric China* from the same publisher. These works provide well-selected illustrations and numerous charts as background to study of the subject.

K. C. Chang's *The Archaeology of Ancient China*, 2nd edition, published by Yale University Press in 1968, is a frequently used single-volume text for prehistoric Chinese studies. The same author's article "The beginnings of agriculture in the Far East," in *Antiquity*, Vol. 44 (1970), pages 175–185, sketches the still incomplete picture of those events. W. Watson's *China Before the Han*, published by Praeger in 1962, and *Early Civilization in China*, published by McGraw-Hill in 1966, are both handy, well-illustrated references. Watson's *Archaeology in China*, published by Parrish in London in 1960, is primarily a book of illustrations, but notes and lengthy captions provide some useful insights. John Hay's *Ancient China*, published by the Bodley Head (London) in 1973, gives brief but well-illustrated references to recent Chinese archaeological finds up to the Tang Dynasty. J. Treistman's *The Prehistory of China: An Archaeological Exploration*, published by Natural History Press in 1972, is the most recent anthropologically oriented account of Chinese prehistory.

Readers interested in the relations between pastoralists and agriculturalists in early China should consult W. Watson's article "The Chinese contribution to Eastern nomad culture in the pre-Han and Han periods" in *World Archaeology*, Vol. 4 (1972), No. 2, as well as Watson's book *Cultural Frontiers in Ancient East Asia*, published in 1971 by the Edinburgh University Press.

An intriguing view of the origins and development of urbanism in China, set in a wide-ranging discourse on world prehistory, is to be found in P. Wheatley's monumental *Pivot of the Four Quarters*, published by Aldine in 1971.

Finally, readers interested in the remarkable Shang and Chou bronzes will encounter a rich literature. Some works providing a basis for further reading include M. Loehr's *Ritual Vessels of Bronze Age*

China, published by Praeger in 1968; Vols. I–V of J. Needham's *Science and Civilization in China,* published by the Cambridge University Press between 1956 and 1963; W. Watson's *Ancient Chinese Bronzes,* published by C. E. Tuttle in 1962; and the article by Hsio-Yen Shih entitled "The study of ancient Chinese bronzes as art and craft," in *World Archaeology,* Vol. 3 (1972), No. 3.

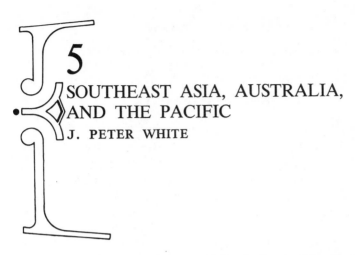

5

SOUTHEAST ASIA, AUSTRALIA, AND THE PACIFIC

J. PETER WHITE

The one-third of the world that is discussed in this chapter includes two extremely distinct zoo-geographical realms—the Oriental and the Australian—as well as the island world of the Pacific.

The Oriental realm includes the countries of Malaya, Thailand, Vietnam, Laos, Cambodia, the Philippines, and Indonesia to the Celebes. These areas are mostly covered with tropical rainforest; among the rich vertebrate fauna are found many placental mammalian types such as dogs, cats, elephants, and primates. The Australian realm consists of the main continent, along with New Guinea, adjacent islands, and Tasmania. Primarily tropical, this area becomes temperate in the south, and has highly distinctive flora. Rats and bats are the only native placental mammals, with unique marsupials filling most of the ecological roles played by other kinds of animals elsewhere. These two realms have been separated for millions of years by the sea barriers of Wallacea, which forms a major bio-geographic boundary. However, many islands within each realm were joined to the mainland masses during periods of lower sea levels in the Pleistocene.

The Pacific islands, such as New Caledonia, Fiji, Tahiti, the Hawaiian Islands, Easter Island, are tropical; New Zealand is an exception. Although impoverished, the land-based fauna and flora are so varied that they can only have been gathered by chance from the surrounding lands during the past few million years.

The prehistory of the entire region is vitally affected by its geography, for only as man's technological sophistication developed

129

could he overcome the problems of moving from west to east in an increasingly maritime environment. There are thus three stages to the region's prehistory: (1) The earliest forms of man are found within the Oriental realm. This is because the area is part of the world's main land mass where man evolved. (2) The Australian realm was settled some time in the Late Pleistocene. This is apparently when man learned to use watercraft and cross ocean barriers of 40–50 miles or more. (3) The Pacific islands were occupied when maritime-oriented societies developed ocean-going vessels, and were sustained by cultivated plants, domestic animals, and sophisticated fishing techniques. This occurred only within the last 5000 years.

Post-settlement contacts throughout the area were also affected by the geography. Changes might spread rapidly overland through most of southeast Asia, but Australia and the Oceanic world could receive them only haphazardly because of the water barriers. Many of the major stimuli for change came from Asia, but these were often altered almost beyond recognition as they passed through the cultural filters of many societies; they were also altered by becoming adapted to the increasingly maritime environment.

The complexities of distribution that were created by the random spread of cultural traits are compounded by the current state of prehistoric research. In general, the quantity and quality of archaeological data decrease from east to west: this is in inverse correlation with land area and time depth. Thus, while the two-thousand-year history of some Polynesian islands is well known, the history of man in Indonesia throughout the Late Pleistocene is almost a blank page. Such gaps in the evidence clearly affect all current interpretations, including the one set out here.

One final complication is that some evidence has been interpreted in the light of theories formulated about the prehistory of other parts of the world, theories which do not fit the data now being discovered. They are therefore often incorrect. This chapter will show how the area discussed here is in certain respects a "third world" with its own developmental characteristics.

The main characteristics currently being investigated by pre-historians, and therefore stressed here in relation to the areas discussed, are: (1) the fact that Pleistocene man in southeast Asia did not develop hand-axe industries, whereas his relatives in Europe, Africa, and India had made hand-axes for perhaps a million years or more; (2) the presence in Australia of the oldest ground stone axes in the world; (3) the probable development of agriculture and the domestication of animals at the same time as in other parts of the world; but the failure of this new economy to spread to Australia; and (4) the highly maritime orientation found among many Pacific peoples, which enabled them to settle, albeit often unintentionally, the scattered islands of the world's largest ocean.

• THE ORIENTAL REALM

Early Men

The earliest hominid remains in this area come from Java, where an australopithecine (often called *Meganthropus paleojavanicus,* but probably a local variant of *Australopithecus robustus*) was found, and may be dated to around two million years ago. These fossils are associated with the Early Pleistocene Djetis fauna, which also includes early forms of the horse, rhinoceros, and elephant. Some *Homo erectus* (sometimes named *Pithecanthropus modjokertensis*) specimens are also said to have been found in the same series of geological deposits (Figure 5.1*A*). The relationship between the two kinds of human fossils is not yet clear, but it is likely that the *H. erectus* fossils are considerably younger than the australopithecine remains. Other *H. erectus* bones, associated with the Middle Pleistocene "Trinil" fauna, have been found in the Kabuh Beds, which are probably 0.5–0.7 million years old.

No definite stone artifacts have yet been recovered from any of these geological horizons although some broken bones, which may represent the remains of meals, have been found in the Upper Kabuh Beds. However, *H. erectus* in Java was probably a stone tool maker, since tools were being made by similar early men in China about the same time, the most common implements being choppers and small scrapers made on flakes. The Patjitanian tool assemblage of Java, which consists of core choppers and chopping tools with alternate flaked edges, and scrapers, points, and perforators made on flakes, is frequently assumed to belong to *H.*

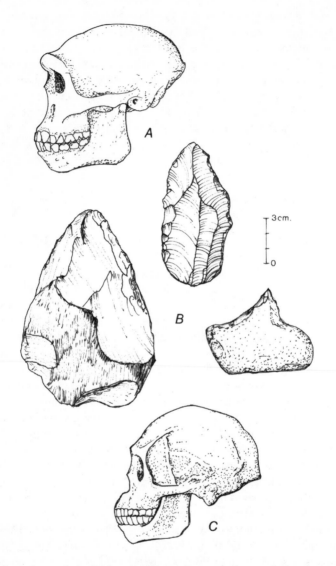

FIGURE 5.1   Paleolithic specimens from southeast Asia, Australia, and the Pacific.   *(A)* Reconstruction of skull of Java Man *(Homo erectus)*.   *(B)* Anyathian, Patjitanian, and Tampanian tools.   *(C)* Reconstruction of skull of Solo Man.

erectus ("Java Man"), although at present the only evidence is from surface collections. The assemblage does not contain true hand-axes. Similar industries without hand-axes have been found in Burma (Anyathian), Malaya (Tampanian), Thailand, China, and West Pakistan. Some Malayan and Chinese specimens have been shown to be of Middle Pleistocene date, making the association of those tools with *H. erectus* more likely. A number of the tool types are shown in Figure 5.1*B*.

These southeast Asian finds show that the technological history of the area throughout the Pleistocene differed from that of Africa and western Eurasia. This is seen particularly in the absence of proper hand-axes, but is also noticeable in the general lack of formal patterning of stone tools.

The absence of hand-axe industries for a period of over a million years in the area east of India has been known for a long time, but no acceptable explanation for it has yet been given. In Africa and western Eurasia, *H. erectus* made millions of hand-axes which were clearly used for many tasks in a wide variety of environments. Many prehistorians consider that the failure to adopt hand-axes in southeast Asia indicates that the area was marginal to human development, but this theory probably places too much stress on stone tools as a sign of human progress. The general absence of formal patterning of stone artifacts may only show that a different technological style was being developed, one that put its formal expression into nonsurviving artifacts, such as wooden tools. Certainly we know from the Choukoutien site (China) that these Asian men used fire, while the presence of large animal bones shows that they were as successful hunters as any people further west. They may have had more simplified stone tools than hand-axes, but they were clearly able to perform the same tasks.

Late Pleistocene Developments
Solo Man, also from Java, may be dated to the Late Pleistocene. Many physical anthropologists think that a family likeness exists between this *Homo sapiens* (*soloensis*) and *Homo erectus,* and that therefore Solo Man may be descended from *H. erectus*. A reconstructed skull of Solo Man is shown in Figure 5.1*C*.

Solo Man continued the technological tradition of *H. erectus,* making crudely flaked and irregular stone scrapers and points. A badly finished bone industry, which was apparently developed about the same time, has also been found. Since both human fossils and artifacts come from geological beds rather than from living sites, the material cannot be integrated easily into temporal and cultural patterns. The Solo skulls are important, though, in providing a temporal link between Java Man and modern man. Most authorities see early man in Australia as being derived from Solo Man.

A wide range of cultural information about the late Pleistocene comes from the Niah cave, which covers several acres in Borneo. This site has been intermittently excavated since 1954, and limited interim reports show that *Homo sapiens* has used the cave since about 40,000 B.C. At that time he made simple core and flake tools as well as a large number of bone points, which presumably were used for spear tips or barbs. Land mammal bones are common in the deposit, but arboreal mammals and birds clearly were not often hunted. It is also interesting to note that only one extinct beast has been found. This suggests that the presence of "modern" faunas cannot necessarily be used, as it is in other parts of the world, to date deposits to the Recent (post-Pleistocene) period.

This evidence, together with the facts that (1) the present distribution of fauna is not greatly different from what it was in the Late Pleistocene, and (2) southeast Pacific Ocean water temperatures are known to have been warm during the last 50,000 years, strongly suggests that there were probably no major climatic changes at the end of the Pleistocene in these tropical areas. This information is useful when discussing the dating of other sites in the region.

An important feature of the Niah excavations is the presence of edge-ground tools made on flaked pebbles, found stratified beneath developed polished axes with round or oval cross-sections. In the deposit between these two types there is a series of transitional forms; these probably also functioned as axes. The earliest edge-ground tools may be dated to around 13,000 B.C. by extrapolation from bracketing radiocarbon dates. Fully ground, round-sectioned axes date from about 6000 B.C. Rather later round axes are found widely in the region in association with pottery, and occur earlier than axes with quadrangular cross-sections.

The presence of edge-ground pebble tools at this very early date of 13,000 B.C., when it is highly unlikely that people anywhere were agriculturalists, shows that any claim for an association between polished axes and agriculture needs to be re-examined. Further, the development from simple edge grinding to well-formed axes at Niah shows that the invention may have occurred independently in this area. Strong confirmation of this comes from the Australian evidence discussed later.

The Tabon caves on Palawan Island in the southern Philippines have produced a flake-tool industry dated to 30,000 B.C. At that time there was a land bridge between the island and Borneo, but there are only general similarities between the material found here and at Niah. The assemblages, dated to between 7000 and 30,000 B.C., consist of flake tools, hammer stones, a few basalt choppers, and animal bones. Most "tools" were simply utilized flakes, the sharp edges of which were used as knives and scrapers. Two trends are visible in the later material: a general reduction in tool size and an increase in the amount of secondary flaking. However, these are not correlated with the economic change caused by rising sea levels which brought marine resources within reach of the caves' inhabitants. There is little other economic evidence, but it seems likely that these people were hunters and gatherers exploiting the varied resources of a defined territory.

There is no evidence at Tabon of the high antiquity of edge grinding found at Niah: the first axes found are made of stone and *Tridacna* clam shell and occur in a fully developed form about 2500 B.C. The absence of early axes may reflect cultural differences between Tabon and Niah, different uses of the two sites, or the failure by archaeologists to recognize early grinding. Or the variation in artifacts may be only a result of the chances of excavation.

The Hoabinhian

The Hoabinhian is an industrial tradition, the earlier phases of which are probably Late Pleistocene in date. It has generally been regarded as "Mesolithic" (that is, post-Pleistocene) since only Recent fauna is found with it, but, as explained above, this method of dating is probably inaccurate here.

The Hoabinhian was originally defined on the basis of excavations in Vietnam in the 1920s and 1930s. Since then, similar industries have been found in south China, Thailand, Laos, Malaya, and Sumatra. Hoabinhian affinities have been claimed for material in Japan, the Philippines, Borneo, and Australia, but the reasoning behind such claims is methodologically unsound. The criteria used to define the Hoabinhian are: (1) unifacial flaked tools made on pebbles and large flakes; (2) "sumatraliths," which are core tools made by completely flaking one side of a pebble; (3) grinding stones, often used for red iron oxide (probably paint); (4) food remains consisting of shellfish, fish, and smaller land mammals; (5) settlements which were either in caves in the uplands, or formed shell middens in coastal areas; (6) the presence of edge grinding on stone tools, and cord-marked pottery in the upper levels of some sites.

The stone technology of this industrial tradition derives from earlier core- and flake-tool traditions in the area rather than from outside it. However, the range and probable time span of the tradition show that several sociocultural groups must be involved, although the lack of detailed excavations and radiocarbon dates prevents these from being defined.

The small, very dry site of Spirit Cave in northwest Thailand is the only Hoabinhian site where modern archaeological techniques have been used to produce detailed economic information. Two main cultural levels have been defined in the 1-meter depth of deposit. The lower cultural level (I) approximately spanned the period 10,000–6500 B.C., while level II was laid down during the next thousand years. Level I contained fairly simple flaked-stone tools of general Hoabinhian type, together with a range of wild animal bones; one bone is possibly from an early form of domestic pig. Also, there is a large number of plant macro-fossils, including a range of nuts used in the area today for food and lighting and as stimulants. A few remains of the bottle gourd, a type of cucumber, Chinese water chestnut, and leguminous beans, all of which possibly represent early domesticated varieties, were also recovered. In other words, the lower level of Spirit Cave seems to indicate that tropical southeast Asia was a third area of the world (along with western Asia and tropical America) where men independently developed agriculture and domesticated animals. This has long been suspected by some geographers.

Level II is marked by the introduction of several new artifact types, notably ground quadrangular-sectioned adzes, slate knives, and cord-marked pottery (Figure 5.2*A*). These features all appear suddenly and in a developed form, so that their evolution must have taken place elsewhere.

Later Hoabinhian materials from Malaya and Thailand are also associated with cord-marked pottery and polished axes, showing that this tradition provided the basis for the development of agricultural societies. Agriculture based on root crops (Figure 5.2*B*) and plants like those of Spirit Cave continued until the spread of rice cultivation around 4000–2500 B.C. resulted in wide cultural change. Detailed excavations of a Corded Ware settlement on Taiwan show it to be considerably earlier than 2500 B.C. In addition to pottery a small number of chipped hoes, some well-polished rectangular adzes, and a number of points were found. Stone knives characteristic of subsequent grain-growing settlements were absent, and neither plant fossils nor animal remains were present to demonstrate conclusively that the settlement was agricultural in character. We would expect people there to be cultivating tubers and fruits, and to have an agricultural system similar to that which diffused into the Pacific.

Much more detailed work is needed before the culture history of this area can be fully written. However, recent work is already changing the traditional picture. For example, there is now definite evidence that pottery was being made in Japan by 10,000 B.C. (Fukui Cave, level III), probably well before the shift to farming; in Thailand there is evidence of copper working by 3000 B.C. (See Figure 5.2*C*.) More work is needed to form a complete picture, but we can see already that the post-Pleistocene developmental history of this area runs parallel to that of western Asia, instead of being derived from it.

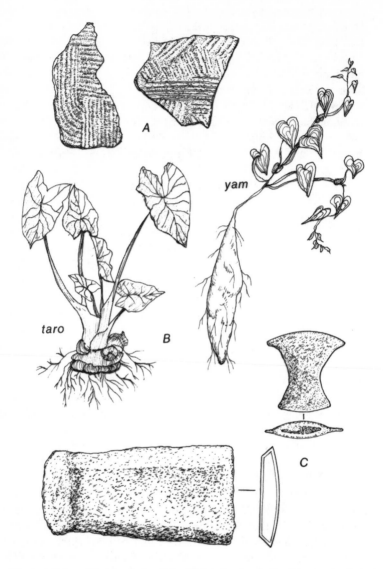

FIGURE 5.2   The period of incipient food production in southeast Asia.   *(A)* Pottery from Spirit Cave.   *(B)* Taro and yam.   *(C)* Copper and bronze artifacts from Non Nok Tha in Thailand.

- THE AUSTRALIAN REALM

Human settlement east of Wallacea began only within the last 50,000 years when man occupied the larger islands of western Melanesia and Australia. Australia and New Guinea were joined into one land mass around 20,000 B.C. by the lowering of sea levels by a maximum of about 450 feet. Some ocean barriers 40–50 miles wide remained, however, in Wallacea and between New Guinea and the islands of the Bismarck Archipelago, and men certainly had watercraft. Settlements from this period and indeed any Late Pleistocene coastal sites are now, of course, under water.

The racial composition of the peoples who settled the Australian realm in Pleistocene and Recent times is not well known. Theories referring to settlements of Negroids, Negritos, Mongoloids, Australoids, Paleo-Melanesians, and so forth, are now known to be based on a limited understanding of human genetic change, but adequate new hypotheses are difficult to form in the absence of evidence of developments through time—especially large, well-dated collections of excavated skeletal material.

Pleistocene Settlement
The earliest definite record of man in the Australian continent comes from the shores of extinct Lake Mungo in the southeast, where a human cremation burial about 25,000 years old has been recently excavated. This skeleton is clearly Aboriginal, although exhibiting some Paleo-Australian features similar to the Talgai and Cohuna skulls. It was found near a campsite where shellfish, fish, birds, and small marsupial mammals were eaten and where stone tools within the early Australian "core tool and scraper" tradition were found. (See Figure 5.3A.)

This "core tool and scraper" tradition is found, with slight variations, throughout Australia until about 5000 B.C. and is similar in a general way to that found until the period of European contact in Tasmania and New Guinea. At Lake Mungo there were tall chunky cores, steep-edge scrapers, and flat scrapers or knives. The shapes of these tools are not highly formalized and it is likely that they were classified by their makers in terms of their working edge,

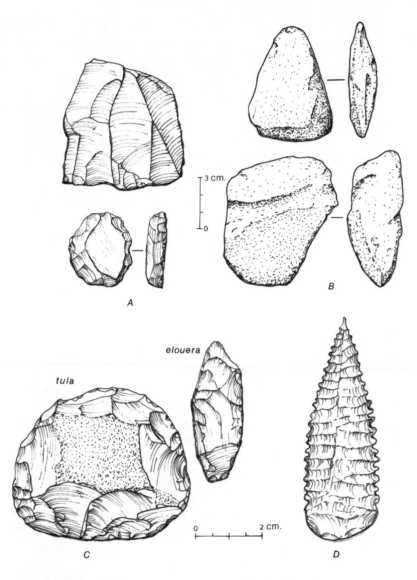

elouera

tula

FIGURE 5.3   Stone artifacts from Australia.   *(A)* Core and scraper
tools.   *(B)* Edge-ground axes.   *(C) Tula* and *elouera*.   *(D)* Kimberley point.

a pattern that may derive from southeast Asian Pleistocene traditions.

The fauna found at Lake Mungo shows the Aborigines to have had an economy very similar to that observed in the area a century ago. The one subsequent addition is seed grinding. The stability of this economy over a time span covering the considerable climatic changes at the end of the Pleistocene is unexpected and interesting when compared to evidence from some other parts of the world. It is worth noting that none of the now-extinct giant marsupials (kangaroos, diprotodonts, and so forth) were found at Lake Mungo, even though it seems that they existed in the area at about this time. This means that it is difficult to assess man's role in their extinction, although it seems likely that he had considerable effect on their life-cycle through hunting and firing the country.

Several other sites dated to earlier than 10,000 B.C. are known in northern and eastern Australia; because of the acid nature of the soil only stone tools have survived in them. A major regional variation which is only now becoming apparent is the presence of ground stone axes as early as 20,000 B.C. in the tropical northern half of the continent. These axes, some of which have hafting grooves for wooden handles, are the oldest ground stone axes in the world, and clearly precede the development of agriculture anywhere. They provide final proof that ground stone tools were not invented by agricultural peoples only, and that the use of "Neolithic" as a technological term must be divorced from such implications. Figure 5.3*B* provides an illustration of these axes.

Unground axes with hafting devices have also been found at the only known Pleistocene site in Melanesia. At Kosipe, in the New Guinea Highlands. seasonal camps were made around 21,000–24,000 B.C. to exploit a large stand of pandanus trees. Only the axes and a few stone flakes were found at this site.

Later evidence comes from cave sites in the New Guinea Highlands. At about 9000 B.C. people made a tool kit consisting of pebble tools, roughly flaked step-flaked scrapers, utilized flakes, and finely ground stone axes of oval or lenticular cross-section. These people were almost certainly hunters and gatherers living off a wide range of small marsupials (the largest animal in New

Guinea weighs less than 150 pounds), nuts, seeds, and roots. Surface collections of similar stone artifacts as well as some linguistic evidence suggest that Late Pleistocene settlement may have extended east to the Bismarck Archipelago and northern Solomon Islands, but no dated archaeological materials yet support this.

Recent Diversity
The post-Pleistocene history of the Australian realm is best discussed in two parts. In Melanesia and Indonesia, the agricultural economy which was developed in southeast Asia by 8000 B.C. was gradually taken up, allowing the development of societies from which the settlements of eastern Melanesia and Polynesia sprung. In Australia, by contrast, hunting and gathering continued. There was a continent-wide change in stone working which did not, however, reach Tasmania.

Australia
The island of Tasmania was the only area of Australia where the original technological pattern continued until European times. This was because Tasmania was isolated from the mainland from about 8000 B.C. onward by the post-glacial sea level rise. Over the last 10,000 years Tasmanians made only minor changes in their stone tools, although they did set up trading systems across the island to supply themselves with better quality stone. They also abandoned the developed bone industry with which they started. More surprisingly, they ceased eating fish about 4000 years ago, while continuing to eat shellfish and marine mammals. The reasons for abandoning such a plentiful protein resource are completely unknown and are difficult even to guess at.

The new technology is found throughout the Australian mainland. It was based on the production of small blades which were used to produce geometric microliths, pointed backed blades, and spearpoints retouched on one or both faces. Small hafted *tula* chisel-adzes and small flakes called *elouera* (Figure 5.3C), used so as to polish one of their unretouched edges, also came into use about the same time. Whether the new technology is a unitary phenomenon, however, is yet to be determined; notable regional differences exist, particularly the general restriction of bifacial points to the north and backed blades to the south of 20° S. latitude. The fact that the oldest dates for backed blades, around 3500 B.C., are found in the interior southeast of Australia, while the oldest bifacial points are dated to about 5000 B.C., also suggests that the backed blades and geometric microliths at least may have been a local invention.

It is not yet clear what socioeconomic changes were associated with this technological change. There is evidence from southern Australia that the introduced dingo, or aboriginal dog, was present around 5000 B.C., whereas this animal's absence in Tasmania suggests that it did not enter Australia before 8000 to 9000 B.C. The two introductions, new stone tools and dingo, may be correlated. It has been argued on similar grounds that spear throwers, boomerangs, and shields were also introduced around 5000 B.C., but there is no archaeological evidence to support this. The absence of axes or adzes in Tasmania cannot be used as a contrary argument, since these tools appear to have been restricted to tropical Australia until brought south with the new technology.

The Pleistocene axes associated with the "core tool and scraper" tradition also demonstrate that the new tools do not, as has been recently suggested, mark the introduction of the concept of hafting stone to make composite tools into Australia. What they do mark is less certain, since there is little evidence to suggest, for example, that they helped man to exploit the environment in new ways. It is possible that there was a change in Aboriginal values at this time; it might have become prestigious to make highly finished stone tools. (Such a change was observed recently in northwestern Australia, where people found the pressure-flaked "Kimberley" spearpoints more aesthetically satisfying. They therefore began to make and use these points even though, in this case, they did not know how to manufacture them properly, and the new weapons were more liable to break than the older type of spearheads. Figure 5.3*D* demonstrates the "aesthetic" nature of the Kimberley point.)

Over time, the second phase of Australian prehistory became regionally diversified. In southeastern Australia specialized stone tools, except for axes, almost completely disappeared by A.D. 1200. They were replaced by miscellaneous trimmed pieces, primary flakes, and bi-polar scalar cores, which were used along with bone points and shell fishhooks. One recent site documents the seasonal exploitation of migrating birds, and similar patterns can be inferred from the ethnographic literature.

In north Australia, where the climate is highly seasonal, one investigation has demonstrated that Aboriginal economic practices remained the same over 7000 years. In the dry season people collected shellfish, waterfowl, and fish, using trident wooden- and bone-tipped spears; in the wet season, man concentrated on hunting large marsupials, using single-pointed stone spears. The contrast between wet and dry seasons is so great that both animals and men have to live alternately in different areas. Different tools and animal remains, deposited by the same people, have therefore been found in the areas. These different archaeological remains might easily have been interpreted as documenting the existence of two geographically distinct subcultures, but this mistake was avoided through the study both of the environment and of the living patterns of Aborigines during the last hundred years. The study of ethnography can provide valuable insights into past patterns of life, especially in Australia, where people remained stone-tool-using hunters and gatherers until the arrival of Europeans.

In spite of contacts with Papuan and Indonesian agricultural peoples along the north coasts of Australia for at least the last thousand years, Aborigines never became agriculturalists. They were, as it happens, never forced into the change, but it is also true that their religion discouraged changes in technology. Aboriginal society stressed the nonmaterial side of life—religion, ritual, and legend were elaborately celebrated in story and by paintings on sand, bark, and stone (Figure 5.4). Perhaps, like many hunter-gatherers, they were simply too well off: the expenditure of labor to collect sufficient food was, in much of the country, less than would have been required by an agricultural system. This was surely true around the monsoonal north coast, where relatively high population densities of 1 person per 2 square miles were common; and this fact would have been sufficient to prevent the acceptance of any introduced economic change, or to prevent its spread to the rest of the continent. Certainly, northern Australia is one of the few areas in the world (like northwest coast America, California,

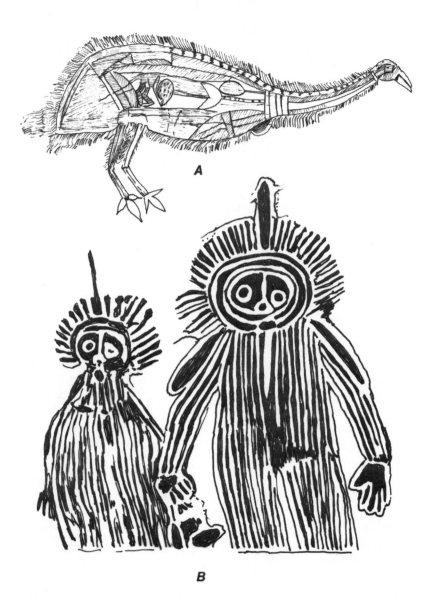

FIGURE 5.4   Australian arts.   (A) Bark painting.   (B) Stone painting.

and southern Africa) that could have supported agriculturalists in prehistoric times but did not. An inquiry into the reasons for this may help us understand why the change did occur in other parts of the world.

Melanesia

Agriculture was adopted in post-Pleistocene times within western Melanesia. However, so little research has been completed that a culture history may be sketched only for the isolated Central Highlands areas of New Guinea. Throughout their history the Highlanders did not take up many of the changes that affected coastal settlements (for example, pottery is unknown in the region), but they were required to adapt the basically tropical living patterns of the lowlands areas to the more temperate climate of the Highlands. Their prehistory is therefore only a limited guide to coastal and island histories.

The first indirect evidence of agriculture in the Highlands is the presence of pig bones in two sites dated to about 4500 B.C. Although the animals have not been proven to be domesticates, it has been assumed that they were, on the grounds that pigs are not native to New Guinea and their introduction by man in a wild form is unlikely. It can then be argued further that *if* these pigs were domesticated, their owners would almost certainly have been agriculturalists, otherwise they would not have been able to produce enough to feed both pigs and themselves. Although this argument is reasonable, it may be challenged in several ways, using ethnographic evidence. Specifically: (1) New Guineans *do* transfer various wild animals such as cassowarys and cuscus from place to place at the present time. (2) Some current New Guinea pig husbandry involves no more than occasionally capturing young feral animals and rearing them for eating. (3) In some lowland areas there are adequate sources of wild foods (for example, sago) which could be used by hunter-gatherers to feed domestic pigs; the Highlands specimens might then simply be feral animals. (4) Many New Guinea peoples now keep only sows and piglets, allowing breeding to occur with feral boars. This means that domestic animals will not be distinguishable from wild ones—and this may always have been true.

These arguments have been spelled out to show some of the difficulties facing prehistorians in this part of the world, and how available ethnographic and archaeological data must be interrelated.

The earliest direct evidence of agriculture in New Guinea is dated to 300 B.C. This consists of a gridiron pattern of prehistoric ditches associated with wooden digging sticks, spades, and stone axes found in the swampy floor of a large Highlands valley. All artifacts, including the ditches, are similar to those currently in use, and it is on this basis that an interpretation of agricultural activity is made. At the time crops probably included taro, yams, bananas, sugarcane (which may be an original New Guinea cultigen), and various local greens.

The most recent major change in the Highlands was the introduction of the sweet potato from America probably via Spanish settlements in the Philippines some 300 years ago, but possibly via Polynesia and Melanesia 500–1000 years ago. This crop, which now forms 90 percent of the diet of most Highlanders, fitted easily into their agricultural system, which was already based on root crops, and gave the same caloric return for less labor input. The technological changes required to adopt this new root crop were minimal.

The chronology of Highland prehistory is confirmed by recent research in Portuguese Timor. The earliest settlements there are dated to about 11,000–12,000 B.C. when hunter-gatherers exploited the only native fauna of giant rats and bats. Pig bones appear around 3500 B.C. along with pottery and shell ornaments. As in New Guinea, this is taken to document an early agricultural phase. Because of its geographic location, Timor continued to be in close contact with southeast Asia, and goats, dogs, and monkeys were brought to the island in the second and third millennia B.C. About 1000 B.C. metal tools began to replace the traditional flint. One major archaeological difference from other areas in this part of the world is the absence of ground stone axes in pre-agricultural contexts, and their scarcity throughout the prehistoric record.

Coastal New Guinea, like Timor, was also in contact with cultures to the west; in this case, the large numbers of people involved, the distances traveled, the variety of local environments, and the widespread existence of large-scale exchange systems lead to many complications in the distributional picture. For instance, recent work in one small area around Port Moresby has produced at least four pottery traditions; between them, they appear to have indirect links throughout Melanesia to Fiji 2200 miles to the east and to Indonesia 2000 miles west. Another example comes from New Ireland, where pottery was made for several hundred years after 500 B.C., but was then given up. The reasons for this are not clear. Alternatively, there is good ethnographic evidence that people in another area learned to make pottery only within the last hundred years, while archaeological evidence suggests that the precise form of the "kula ring" exchange system, as defined by Malinowski, may be only a recent phenomenon. At present, however, we can write no consistent story from clues of this kind.

The study of present-day languages and their distribution can also provide important prehistoric data, though this is often difficult to correlate with archaeology. Within Melanesia there are two main language groups, the Austronesian and the Papuan (non-Austronesian). Papuan languages occur primarily in New Guinea, especially inland, and in the Bismarck Archipelago, with a few representatives as far east as the Solomon Islands. These languages are very diverse and only very distantly related among themselves. Their only known relatives outside Melanesia are in Timor. Austronesian languages occur only in lowland (mostly coastal) areas of the New Guinea mainland; they are part of a family found scattered through island Melanesia, Indonesia, parts of southeast Asia, Madagascar, and throughout Micronesia and Polynesia. The Austronesian languages of parts of Melanesia and Polynesia are quite closely related. Historical linguists argue from these facts that Papuan languages are the earlier ones in Melanesia and Timor, and that they were replaced in coastal and island areas by Austronesian, probably partly as a result of migrations around 4000–6000 B.C. It was from among Austronesian speakers in the New Guinea-Bismarck region (where there is the greatest concentration of the most diverse languages, and hence presumably the greatest time-depth) that the settlers of the rest of the Pacific came. On the basis of common words it can be shown that the early Austronesian speakers lived in stone age, agricultural communities. They grew taro and bananas, kept pigs, and were considerable fishermen and sailors. They were also potters, and nearly all Melanesian pottery-making societies today speak Austronesian languages.

Linguists are sharply divided between those who regard Austronesian as immigrating to Melanesia from southeast Asia, and those who see it as originating in the area. Nonetheless, it is clear that in general, the linguistic and archaeological accounts of prehistory are similar, although archaeological definitions of Austronesian-speaking groups have yet to be made. One proposed link, Lapita pottery, will be discussed here.

Micronesia

Little is known of the prehistory of the Micronesian islands. There is evidence of agricultural settlements with pottery and stone and shell adzes on some islands by 1500 B.C., and with massive stone house foundations and new types of pottery occurring on Saipan by A.D. 750. Micronesian languages belong to the Austronesian family, but neither their internal relationships nor their links with Polynesian and Melanesian are clear. There is little reason to believe that the primary settlement of the Pacific came through Micronesia, although many styles of oceanic fishing equipment which were derived from Japan and the North Pacific must have been diffused via the area. Micronesian culture was highly oceanic in orientation, and 300-mile voyages using canoes and traditional navigation methods are known.

• THE PACIFIC ISLANDS

The Lapita Tradition

The smaller islands of eastern Melanesia and Polynesia were settled in the period 2000 B.C.–A.D. 1000 by agriculturalists and husbandmen with a strongly maritime cultural orientation. One archaeological expression of this settlement appears to be represented by the Lapita pottery tradition.

Lapita pottery (Figure 5.5*A*) is named after a site in New Caledonia. It is distinguished by its decoration which consists of carefully applied bands of repetitive geometrics that are made by means of a very fine-toothed stamp around the body of the vessel.

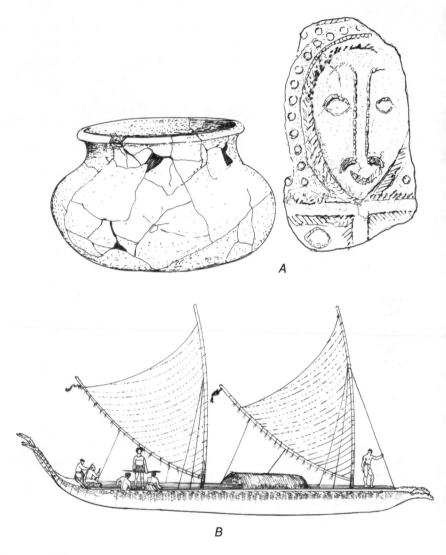

FIGURE 5.5   Oceanian culture.   (A) Lapita pot and motif.   (B) Polynesian canoe.

This highly decorated pottery is found on sites from the Bismarck Archipelago through the New Hebrides, New Caledonia, and Fiji, and as far east as Tonga in western Polynesia. It is the earliest pottery in Fiji (around 1200 B.C.) and the only pottery in Tonga (1100–200 B.C.), but it occurs at the same time as other decorative traditions (incised, paddle decorated) further west. There is a difference of only 500 years in the first appearance of Lapita ware throughout the area.

The maritime regime of the Lapita potters is underscored by their site locations. From the Bismarck Archipelago to New Caledonia, Lapita sites are found on small offshore islands or beach sites with some landward protection. Even in Fiji most sites are near the sea, and only on the small island of Tonga are both inland and coastal sites known.

Artifacts associated with Lapita pottery in Tonga, where the tradition is best known, include stone adzes, shell adzes, scrapers, knives, chisels, octopus lures, and net sinkers, as well as a few bone needles and awls. Most bracelets, beads, and pendants were made of shell. Some of these artifacts are similar to those found on Lapita sites further west, especially stone and shell adzes, chisels, and bracelets, shell food-scrapers, and beads. The bones of domesticated pig, dog, and chicken as well as fish and shellfish were also found.

It is clear that people making Lapita pottery were among the cultural groups that combined in some way to become Polynesians, for many items within early Tongan material culture also appear further east. On the other hand, the pottery, certain stone adze types, and some shell artifacts found in the rest of Polynesia, including nearby Samoa, are already different from Tongan material culture as early as A.D. 100. This suggests that a complex process of intergroup trading and movement must have been a feature of the area from the time of first settlement.

Similar movements, some involving quite large numbers of people, between the closely spaced islands of eastern Melanesia constitute a continuing feature of their history, if ethnographic and ethnohistorical records are any guide. Trade, warfare, and migration, which produce complex and often apparently random distributions, insured that new pottery types, adze forms, and shell decorations were established at only some points through the area. This situation arises because a canoe (Figure 5.5*B*) may voyage 200 miles nearly as easily as 20 miles, allowing inhospitable areas to be bypassed in a way that is not always possible on land. In some ways prehistorians are fortunate that eastern Polynesia was settled only within the last 2000 years!

Polynesia
Polynesians are popularly believed to have settled the islands from Hawaii to New Zealand by means of planned and carefully navigated voyages, with subsequent voyages being undertaken to maintain interisland contact. Some people also believe that the Kon-Tiki raft voyage showed that eastern Polynesia, at least, was settled from the Americas. Neither of these beliefs is true.

In regard to possible American settlement it can be shown in detail that the languages, racial groups, material culture, agricultural methods, animals (both domesticated, and wild rats and lizards), and nearly all crop plants of Polynesia derive from the *west*. The most significant case for contact between Polynesia and the Americas is the pre-European presence of the sweet potato in eastern Polynesia: there is little doubt that this is an American plant and that it must have been transferred by humans. Such contact, however, was probably a chance matter, since no other significant cultural materials were transferred. The most likely American area from which voyages might have come is around the Gulf of Guayaquil (Ecuador); the most likely time is 100 B.C.–A.D. 400. Alternatively, a stray Polynesian boat might have reached America and returned at any time.

The matter of Polynesian voyaging is more complicated. At the time of European contact Polynesians were highly competent sailors using traditional methods of navigation to make deliberate voyages of more than 200 miles between islands for purposes of trade or war. At the same time there are many records of accidental journeys made by canoes blown off course and becoming lost. No deliberate voyages involving straight runs of more than 500 miles with a subsequent return have been recorded, and traditions that refer to such travels all make use of knowledge gained through European contact. Thus, while there was continuous voyaging between such island groups as the Societies and the Tuamotus, and within those such as the southern Cooks, Tonga-Samoa, and Tonga-Fiji, the more isolated islands—Hawaii, Easter, New Zealand, and so forth—were discovered only by chance and thereafter isolated, except for further chance arrivals. Given that Polynesian languages are mutually intelligible, later chance arrivals, such as a well-equipped group of political exiles, might easily have been important in the history of smaller islands. But their arrival would have been accidental and not deliberate. The random nature of Polynesian settlement is further supported by the varied omissions from basic Polynesian material culture on each island: pigs in Mangareva, Easter Island, Niue, and New Zealand; fowls in New Zealand; the *fe'i* banana in the Hawaiian Islands; and so on.

The precise order of settlement from the central dispersal area, normally assumed to be the Society Islands, is still in dispute and may never be entirely clear. We know that the Polynesian islands were peopled by a single race who depended upon sweet potato, taro, breadfruit, and banana agriculture, sometimes kept pigs and dogs, and relied on fish and shellfish for much of their protein. The quality of life varied according to whether the island was an atoll with poor soil, or a high, rich volcanic island. Surprisingly, no eastern Polynesians were potters. The one major variation in this total picture is found in New Zealand where, as in the New Guinea Highlands, a basically tropical culture was adapted to a more temperate climate.

The initial settlement of New Zealand occurred around A.D. 500–750 at the extreme north end of North Island, where tropical style agriculture was still possible. People moved from here into cooler regions where moa birds (now extinct) were hunted in large numbers and a coastal food-collecting economy was established. The gradual discovery of new propagation techniques and storage methods for the sweet potato then allowed agricultural activity to spread some distance further south. However, fern root and other native plants were still collected for food in many areas. The limited areas of high-resource potential led to concentrations of population, fostering social stratification, intergroup conflict, and the development of massive earth fortifications (*pa*), especially in the fifteenth century and later. The classic Maori culture, first reported in Europe by Captain Cook, developed only at this time.

• BIBLIOGRAPHIC ESSAY

The most recent summary of archaeological work in southeast Asia is contained in an article by I. C. Glover entitled "Late Stone Age traditions in South-East Asia," which appears in the volume *South Asian Archaeology,* edited by N. Hammond and published by Duckworth (London) in 1973. Other chapters in the same volume provide the interested reader with information about neighboring culture areas.

A spirited article by C. Gorman entitled "The Hoabinhian and after: subsistence patterns in southeast Asia during the Late Pleistocene and Early Recent periods," appearing in *World Archaeology,* Vol. 2 (1971), No. 3, and a slightly less technical account by J. Golson, "The remarkable history of Indo-Pacific man: missing chapters from every world prehistory," in *Search,* Vol. 3 (1972), pages 3–21, also serve to shed light on this archaeologically long neglected part of Asia. An article by W. G. Solheim II, entitled "An earlier agricultural revolution," published in *Scientific American,* April 1972, presents the somewhat controversial evidence for an early indigenous development of food production in southeast Asia.

D. J. Mulvaney's book *The Prehistory of Australia,* published by Thames and Hudson (London) in 1969, provides a basic archaeological framework for the continent. It may be read profitably in conjunction with the work *Aboriginal Man and Environment in Australia,* edited by Mulvaney and J. Golson, published by Australian National University Press in 1971. This collection combines essays on Australian geomorphology, paleo-ecology, Aboriginal linguistics, ethnology, and physical anthropology with archaeological reports, and the volume deserves the careful attention of all those interested in Australian prehistory. R. Gould's work *Australian Archaeology in Ecological and Ethnographic Perspective,* a Warner Modular Publication in Anthropology, No. 7, 1973, provides a convenient, up-to-date view of the state of Australian archaeology and its opportunities for development, in conjunction with studies of the Australian environment and modern Aboriginal population.

R. Green and M. Kelly's edited collection, *Studies in Oceanic Culture History*, published in Honolulu in two volumes as Nos. 11 and 12 in the B. P. Bishop Museum's Pacific Anthropological Records series, 1970–71, provides a recent overview of Melanesian and Polynesian archaeology. Other volumes in that same series also contain reports of excavation and survey in Oceania. *Polynesian Culture History*, edited by G. A. Highland et al., and published by the B. P. Bishop Museum in 1968, provides a useful background to the above-mentioned volumes edited by Green and Kelly.

COMPLETE BIBLIOGRAPHY

This bibliography lists all the sources referred to in the bibliographic essays after the individual chapters. Together the readings provide a good sampling of the literature.

Alexander, J., 1965, *Jugoslavia Before the Roman Conquest,* Thames and Hudson, London.

Barfield, L., 1972, *Northern Italy Before Rome,* Thames and Hudson, London.

Bernac, A., 1963, *Troy and the Trojans,* Thames and Hudson, London.

Blumenstock, D., 1966, *Pleistocene and Post-Pleistocene Climatic Variations in the Pacific Area,* University of Hawaii Press, Honolulu.

Bradley, R., 1972, "Prehistorians and Pastoralists in Neolithic and Bronze Age England," *World Archaeology,* Vol. 4, No. 2.

Brea, L. B., 1966, *Sicily,* Thames and Hudson, London.

Butzer, K. W., 1971, *Environment and Archaeology* (2nd edition), Aldine, Chicago.

Caskey, J. L., 1959, "Activities at Lerna," *Hesperia,* Vol. 28, pp. 202–207.

————, 1971, "Greece, Crete, and the Aegean Islands in the Early Bronze Age," *Cambridge Ancient History,* Vol. I, Part II, Cambridge University Press, Cambridge, England.

Chadwick, N., 1971, *The Celts,* Penguin, New York and Harmondsworth, Middlesex, England.

Chang, K. C., 1968, *The Archaeology of Ancient China* (2nd edition), Yale University Press, New Haven.

157

————, 1970, "The Beginnings of Agriculture in the Far East," *Antiquity,* Vol. 44, pp. 175–185.

Chêng, T. K., 1963, *Chou China,* Heffer and Sons, Cambridge, England.

————, 1966, *New Light on Prehistoric China,* Heffer and Sons, Cambridge, England.

————, 1959, *Prehistoric China,* Heffer and Sons, Cambridge, England.

————, 1960, *Shang China,* Heffer and Sons, Cambridge, England.

Childe, V. G., 1957, *Dawn of European Civilization* (6th edition), Routledge and Kegan Paul, London.

Clark, J. D., 1963, *Prehistoric Cultures of Northeast Angola and Their Significance in Tropical Africa,* Museo do Dundo, Lisbon.

————, 1970, *The Prehistory of Africa,* Thames and Hudson, London. Paperback, Praeger, New York.

————, 1959, *The Prehistory of Southern Africa,* Pelican, London.

Clark, J. G. D., 1954, *Excavations at Star Carr,* Cambridge University Press, Cambridge, England.

————, 1952, *Prehistoric Europe: The Economic Basis,* Stanford University Press, Stanford.

————, 1972, *Star Carr: A Case Study in Bio-archaeology,* Addison-Wesley Module in Anthropology, No. 10, Reading, Massachusetts.

Cole, S., 1963, *The Prehistory of East Africa,* Macmillan, London.

Courtin, J., 1972, *Le Néolithique de la Provence,* Centre National de la Recherche Scientifique, Paris.

Daniel, G., 1958, *The Megalith Builders of Western Europe,* Hutchinson, London.

Davidson, B., 1960, *Old Africa Rediscovered,* Gollancz, London.

Davies, O., 1967, *West Africa Before the Europeans,* Methuen, London.

Escalen de Fontan, M., 1966, "Du Paléolithique Supérieur au Mésolithique dans le Midi Méditerranéen," *Bulletin de la Société Préhistorique Française,* Vol. 62, Fasc. 1, pp. 50–66, Paris.

Evans, J. D., 1964, "Excavations in the Neolithic Mound of Knossos, 1958–60," *Bulletin of the Institute of Archaeology of the University of London,* Vol. 66, pp. 4–34.

————, 1971, *Prehistoric Antiquities of the Maltese Islands,* Athlone, London.

Fage, J. D., and R. A. Oliver, editors, 1970, *Papers in African Prehistory,* Cambridge University Press, Cambridge, England.

Flint, R. F., 1971, *Glacial and Quaternary Geology,* Wiley, New York.

Gimbutas, M., 1965, *Bronze Age Cultures in Central and Eastern Europe,* Mouton, The Hague.

Glover, I. C., 1973, "Late Stone Age Traditions in South-East Asia," *South Asian Archaeology,* N. Hammond, editor, Duckworth, London.

Golson, J., 1972, "The Remarkable History of Indo-Pacific Man: Missing Chapters from Every World Prehistory," *Search,* Vol. 3, pp. 3–21.

Gorman, C., 1971, "The Hoabinhian and After: Subsistence Patterns in Southeast Asia During the Late Pleistocene and Early Recent Periods," *World Archaeology,* Vol. 2, No. 3.

Gould, R., 1973, *Australian Archaeology in Ecological and Ethnographic Perspective,* Warner Modular Publication in Anthropology, No. 7, Andover, Massachusetts.

Green, R., and M. Kelly, editors, 1970–1971, *Studies in Oceanic Culture History,* 2 vols., Pacific Anthropological Records, Nos. 11–12, B. P. Bishop Museum, Honolulu.

Hay, J., 1973, *Ancient China,* Bodley Head, London.

Herrman, A., 1966, *An Historical Atlas of China,* Aldine, Chicago.

Higgs, E. S., and C. Vita-Finzi, 1965–1967, "The Climate, Environment and Industries of Stone Age Greece," *Proceedings of the Prehistoric Society,* Parts I–III, London.

Highland, G. A., et al., 1968, *Polynesian Culture History,* B. P. Bishop Museum, Honolulu.

Howell, F. C., 1965, *Early Man,* Time-Life Books, New York.

Hutchinson, R. W., 1962, *Prehistoric Crete,* Penguin, Harmondsworth, Middlesex, England.

Isaac, G. L., 1971, "The Diet of Early Man: Aspects of Archaeological Evidence from Lower and Middle Pleistocene Sites in Africa," *World Archaeology,* Vol. 2, No. 3.

———, 1969, "Studies of Early Culture in East Africa," *World Archaeology,* Vol. 1, No. 1.

Jarman, M., 1971, "Culture and Economy in the North Italian Neolithic," *World Archaeology,* Vol. 2, No. 3.

Kurten, B., 1968, *Pleistocene Mammals of Europe,* Aldine, Chicago.

Loehr, M., 1968, *Ritual Vessels of Bronze Age China,* Praeger, New York.

McBurney, C. B. M., 1960, *The Stone Age of Northern Africa,* Penguin, Harmondsworth, Middlesex, England.

Michael, H. N., editor, 1964, *The Archaeology and Geomorphology of Northern Asia,* Arctic Institute of North America, Washington, D.C.

Mulvaney, D. J., 1969, *The Prehistory of Australia,* Thames and Hudson, London.

————, and J. Golson, editors, 1971, *Aboriginal Man and Environment in Australia,* Australian National University Press, Canberra.

Murray, J., 1970, *The First European Agriculture,* Edinburgh University Press, Edinburgh.

Needham, J., 1956–1963, *Science and Civilization in China,* Vols. I–V, Cambridge University Press, Cambridge, England.

Olsson, I. U., editor, 1970, *Radiocarbon Variations and Absolute Chronology,* Wiley, New York.

Pericot-Garcia, L., 1972, *The Balearic Islands,* Thames and Hudson, London.

Phillips, P., 1972, "Population, Economy, and Society in the Chassey-Cortaillod-Lagozza Cultures," *World Archaeology,* Vol. 4, No. 1.

Piggott, S., 1965, *Ancient Europe,* Edinburgh University Press, Edinburgh.

————, 1954, *Neolithic Cultures of the British Isles,* Cambridge University Press, Cambridge, England.

————, G. Daniel, and C. McBurney, editors, 1974, *France Before the Romans,* Thames and Hudson, London.

Renfrew, C., 1973, *Before Civilization,* Knopf, New York.

————, 1967, "Colonialism and Megalithismus," *Antiquity,* Vol. 41, pp. 276–288.

————, 1972, *The Emergence of Civilisation: The Cyclades and the Aegean in the Third Millenium B.C.,* Methuen, London.

————, editor, 1973, *The Explanation of Culture Change: Models in Prehistory,* University of Pittsburgh Press, Pittsburgh.

————, 1973, "Monuments, Mobilization and Social Organization," *The Explanation of Culture Change: Models in Prehistory,* C. Renfrew, editor, University of Pittsburgh Press, Pittsburgh.

Renfrew, J. M., 1973, *Palaeoethnobotany,* Columbia University Press, New York.

Rodden, R., 1965, "An Early Neolithic Village in Greece," *Scientific American,* April.

————, 1964, "A European Link with Chatal Huyuk, Uncovering a Seventh Millenium Site in Macedonia, Part I," *Illustrated London News,* 11 April, pp. 564–567.

————, 1964, "A European Link with Chatal Huyuk, Uncovering a

Seventh Millennium Site in Macedonia, Part II, Burials and Shrines," *Illustrated London News,* 18 April, pp. 604–607.

———, 1962, "Excavations at the Early Neolithic Site of Nea Nikomedia," *Proceedings of the Prehistoric Society,* Vol. 28, pp. 267–288, London.

Rust, A., 1937, *Das Altsteinzeitliche Rentierjägerlager Meiendorf,* K. Wachholtz, Neumünster, West Germany.

———, 1943, *Die Alt- und Mittelsteinzeitlichen Funde von Stellmoor,* K. Wachholtz, Neumünster, West Germany.

Sampson, C. G., 1974, *The Stone Age in Southern Africa,* Academic Press, New York.

Shih, H.-Y., 1972, "The Study of Ancient Chinese Bronzes as Art and Craft," *World Archaeology,* Vol. 3, No. 3.

Shinnie, P. L., editor, 1971, *The African Iron Age,* Clarendon Press, Oxford.

Solheim II, W. G., 1972, "An Earlier Agricultural Revolution," *Scientific American,* April.

Soudsky, B., 1962, "The Neolithic Site of Bylany," *Antiquity,* Vol. 36, pp. 190–200.

———, and I. Pavlu, 1971, "The Linear Pottery Culture Settlement Patterns of Central Europe," *Man, Settlement and Urbanism,* P. Ucko, R. Tringham, and G. Dimbleby, editors, Duckworth, London.

Srejović, D., 1966, "Lepenski Vir—A New Prehistoric Culture in the Danubian Region," *Archeologica Iugoslavica,* Vol. 7, pp. 13–18, Belgrade.

Stubbings, F. H., 1972, *Prehistoric Greece,* Rupert Hart-Davis, London.

Taylor, W., 1964, *The Mycenaeans,* Thames and Hudson, London.

Treistman, J., 1972, *The Prehistory of China: An Archaeological Exploration,* Natural History Press, New York.

Tringham, R., 1971, *Hunters, Fishers, and Farmers of Eastern Europe: 6000–3000 B.C.,* Hutchinson, London.

Trump, D., 1966, *Central and Southern Italy Before Rome,* Thames and Hudson, London.

Vita-Finzi, C., 1972, *The Mediterranean Valleys: Geological Changes in Historic Times,* Cambridge University Press, Cambridge, England.

Watson, W., 1962, *Ancient Chinese Bronzes,* C. E. Tuttle, Rutland, Vermont.

———, 1960, *Archaeology in China,* Parrish, London.

162   *Varieties of Culture in the Old World*

————, 1962, *China Before the Han,* Praeger, New York.

————, 1972, "The Chinese Contribution to Eastern Nomad Culture in the pre-Han and Han Periods," *World Archaeology,* Vol. 4, No. 2.

————, 1971, *Cultural Frontiers in Ancient East Asia,* Edinburgh University Press, Edinburgh.

————, 1966, *Early Civilization in China,* McGraw-Hill, New York.

Wheatley, P., 1971, *Pivot of the Four Quarters,* Aldine, Chicago.

Whitehouse, R., 1971, "The Last Hunter-Gatherers in Southern Italy," *World Archaeology,* Vol. 2, No. 3.

INDEX

NOTE: References to illustrations are in *italics*.

163